T0283974

OHIO
—— AT ——
ANTIETAM

The Buckeye State's Sacrifice on America's Bloodiest Day

KEVIN R. PAWLAK AND DAN WELCH

THE
History
PRESS

Published by The History Press
Charleston, SC
www.historypress.com

Battle of Antietam, by Kurz and Allison, 1888. *Courtesy of the Library of Congress.*

First published 2021

Manufactured in the United States

ISBN 9781467146913

Library of Congress Control Number: 2021938394

To Ohio's soldiers who served in the Maryland Campaign.
"Not for themselves, but for their country."

Contents

Acknowledgements

W e first wish to sincerely thank our editor at The History Press, John Rodrigue. John graciously guided us through the ups and downs of writing this book. Researching and acquiring images during the pandemic was not an easy task. John was always willing to be flexible with us and lend a helping hand. Ashley Hill, likewise, offered helpful comments to improve the manuscript.

Many people kindly gave us their time to help make this book possible. Edward Alexander created the maps depicting the actions of Ohioans at South Mountain and Antietam. Tom Clemens provided sources and help along the way. Specifically, he helped answer the question about where Ewing's brigade crossed Antietam Creek on September 17, 1862. Steve Stotelmyer, likewise, lent us assistance.

A host of people and organizations have preserved the stories of Ohioans during the Maryland Campaign. Julie Mayle and the staff at the Rutherford B. Hayes Presidential Library digitized many previously unpublished images for this book. Jenni Salamon and the staff at the Ohio Historical Society provided images of the battle flags found in this book. Jon Tracey braved a cold winter's day to take photographs of headstones in Antietam National Cemetery. Leight Murray of Marietta, Ohio, took numerous modern-day images of notable Ohioans' homes and the final resting places of those who served at Antietam. Larry Strayer agreed to provide a hard-to-find image of Melvin Clarke, an image and story crucial to the manuscript. Mike Peters of Pickerington, Ohio, provided digitized versions of several hard to find primary sources. Mike also put us in touch with several other private collectors, thereby expanding the visual aspects of this work. Ron Davidson at the Sandusky Library also provided another crucial image that was necessary to give a face to an important story in the manuscript. Linda Showalter at Marietta College aided us in conducting research and digitizing images. Stephanie Gray at Antietam National Battlefield was always willing to let us research in the park's library. Jennifer Loredo at the United States Army Heritage and Education Center supplied us with images from the indispensable MOLLUS Collection.

Though many people pushed this book across the finish line to the printers, any mistakes or errors are entirely our own.

Lastly, we could not have written this book without the Ohioans who participated in the Maryland Campaign and extensively wrote about their experiences. It is to them that we dedicate this book. Without their efforts to preserve and share what they saw, felt and thought in September 1862, this book would have been impossible to write.

INTRODUCTION

The federal war effort during the American Civil War was truly a united endeavor. It was a geographic collective of states that believed in the preservation of the Union, the end of slavery and the need to suppress an open rebellion within the country. States as far away from each other as Maine and Wisconsin, Rhode Island and Minnesota, all came together to accomplish the strategic and ideological goals of the United States government between 1861 and 1865. The state of Ohio was among those states willing to offer its men, material and money to this effort—and it was one of the earliest to do so.

On January 7, 1861, just two and a half weeks after South Carolina declared its secession from the United States, the Ohio General Assembly met and loudly proclaimed the state's feelings toward rebellion, secession and war. State senator Richard A. Harrison offered a number of resolutions that were then adopted by both houses of the state legislature. These resolutions noted, in part: "The people of Ohio believe [in] the preservation of this government" and that "the general government cannot permit the secession of any state without violating the bond and compact of the Union." Furthermore, they stated, "The power of the national government must be maintained." Despite these early proclamations from the Ohio legislature positioning the state in the then-current sectional crisis, there were still aspects of the southern states' constitutional and political ideologies that Ohio still agreed with.[1]

"The people of Ohio are opposed to meddling with the internal affairs of other states," the resolution stated. Thus, these Ohio state congressmen believed in the concept of state's rights and Ohio's desire not to interfere. Furthermore, one of the resolutions went so far as to support the Fugitive Slave Law and the repeal of any state laws that had been passed in opposition to it being carried out by those states' citizens. These parts of the resolution horrified the numerous abolitionists within the state. Even though these aspects did not align with all of the northern states' political and constitutional ideologies, as the secession crisis moved further into the winter of 1861, the Ohio state legislature felt strongly about what it had passed. Copies were sent out to President Buchanan, both the U.S. House of Representatives and Senate and even the governors of all the states that were still in the Union.[2]

Although Ohio came out strong against South Carolina quickly after its secession ordinance, that did not mean it wanted to send its sons into battle if it could be avoided. When the Virginia legislature sent out a call for a peace convention in Washington, D.C., the Ohio General Assembly sent seven prominent Ohioians to the meeting on February 4, 1861. The conference ended in failure. And events continued to hurdle rapidly toward war. On April 12, 1861, an Ohio state senator rushed into the chamber. After catching his breath, he yelled out, "Mr. President, the telegraph announces that the secessionists are bombarding Fort Sumter!" The chamber fell silent. Abby Kelley Foster, an abolitionist who was in the gallery that day to hear arguments on the expansion of legal rights of married women, cried out, "Thank God!" It was not long before news of Fort Sumter's surrender reached the chamber, and on April 15, President Lincoln called for seventy-five thousand volunteers. Governor William Dennison immediately asked President Lincoln what Ohio's quota would be of that number. "What proportion of the 75,000 militia you call do you give Ohio?" Dennison wrote. "We will furnish the largest number you will receive. Great rejoicing here over your proclamation." Ohio's quota was 13,000 men. Overnight, Ohio transformed onto a war footing.[3]

Within twenty-four hours of Lincoln's call, the state appropriated $1 million to arm and equip these men and prepare for a defense. Soon, another $1.5 million was set aside in case of an invasion into the state. In addition to these funds, a tax was voted in the affirmative with the express purpose of providing economic relief to families of those men who volunteered for service. If this sum of money being spent on the new war effort astonished Ohioians in April 1861, it would prove to be just a miniscule amount of the total spent by April 1865 and beyond.[4]

Ohio mobilized quickly. Martin Andrews wrote to the governor on April 15, "Within a week, a wonderful change has taken place....Now, it is no longer Republicans or Democrats but the *people*...[and they] are ready with men and money." Just seven days after that senator had announced the news of Fort Sumter on the chamber floor, approximately two thousand soldiers of the First and Second Ohio Volunteer Infantry were on their way to the growing defenses of Washington, D.C. This was only the beginning of Ohio's commitment of blood and treasure to the war effort. After all, Ohio had a lot to give. In 1860, the state ranked third among the northern states in both population and wealth.[5]

Following the conclusion of the war, as official reports and correspondence were accumulated, reflections on Ohio's contributions became clear. Between 1861 and 1865, Ohio had contributed 319,189 men to the war effort, of which, 35,475 gave "their last full measure of devotion." Further information collected from wartime records revealed that 3 of every 5 male Ohioans between the ages of eighteen and forty-five had served in the Civil War. Only two other states put more of their military-aged men in the field: New York and Pennsylvania. But with respect to the proportion those men comprised of the entire state population, among northern states, Ohio led the way. In total, Ohio sent 230 infantry and cavalry regiments, 26 independent batteries of artillery and 5 independent companies of sharpshooters to the front. Additionally, 3,452 Ohioans served on gunboats, and 5,092 Ohio freedmen served in the various branches of the federal armies. To entice Ohioans to serve, the state made sure the men in the ranks from Ohio were well compensated. In addition to regular army pay and premiums, Ohio spent $23,500,000 on local bounties. Not every man volunteered, nor did every man stay to his post, however. Because of the strong, patriotic fervor that Ohioans brought with them into the war effort only 8,750 were drafted for service and fewer than 44 Ohioians per thousand deserted, an astonishingly low rate among the northern states.[6]

Ohio had mobilized for war. As the weeks, months and years of the war continued to drag on, Ohio's men fought and spilt blood on almost every major battlefield and in numerous other skirmishes and engagements. Included in this list would be America's single bloodiest day: September 17, 1862. Ohio and its sons played a vital role in the Maryland Campaign in the summer of 1862, and they saw heavy fighting at South Mountain and in the fields around Sharpsburg. The stories of bravery, gallantry and sacrifice from these units and men have filled various publications since the campaign's close. They can be found in contemporary newspapers, letters and diaries. During the postwar era, more could be found in regimental and unit histories, often written by the veterans of these units themselves. Previously unpublished or obscure sources were found, brought to light and published during the twentieth century.

Found among the pages of this book will be some of those familiar accounts, interpreted and told with new voices and perspectives. But for many, this work will include stories and accounts of Ohioans that have long since been forgotten or were previously untold. We hope that *Ohio at Antietam* will "remind this generation of the debt it owes to the soldiers who won the victory for the Union, not only for themselves, but for the millions who enjoy the fruits of the triumph gained at the cost of so many thousands of lives."[7]

1

"HAVE YOUR MEN READY TO MARCH"

Ohioans to Antietam

L ieutenant Colonel Rutherford B. Hayes and the men under his
  command in the Twenty-Third Ohio Infantry had been in the vicinity
of Washington, D.C., less than two weeks before embarking on the Maryland
Campaign in September 1862. They came east with the other regiments
of the Kanawha Division from western Virginia. Hayes called their then-
current location outside the nation's capital "the critical region." He and his
men were no doubt eager to show the Army of the Potomac and the Army
of Northern Virginia their fighting mettle.[8]

When Brigadier General Jacob Cox's all-Ohio infantry, Kanawha
Division, reached Washington, D.C., "great were the expectations of seeing
military life in its most finished and scientific forms," remembered the
Eleventh Ohio Infantry's chaplain, William Lyle. Lyle and his comrades
read in newspapers of the eastern army's "efficiency in all military duties,
its perfect discipline, and its unbounded confidence in its leaders." These
Ohioans found a different picture when they arrived in Washington, D.C.,
and saw its defenses. "It seemed as if order and discipline existed nowhere,"
recalled Lyle.[9]

Union troops were flooding into Washington from all directions by the end
of August 1862. The Fourth and Eighth Ohio Infantry Regiments, part of the
Army of the Potomac's Second Corps, arrived from the Virginia Peninsula.
Ohio's Fifth, Seventh, Twenty-Ninth and Sixty-Sixth Infantry Regiments
were part of the Army of Virginia's Second Corps, which became the Twelfth
Corps of the Army of the Potomac during the Maryland Campaign. Cox's

Kanawha Division, which consisted of the Eleventh, Twelfth, Twenty-Third, Twenty-Eighth, Thirtieth and Thirty-Sixth Ohio Infantry Regiments, came from western Virginia and was part of the Ninth Corps.[10]

Despite the two recent setbacks on the Peninsula and at the Battle of Second Bull Run, the Union forces gathered around Washington and received a morale boost in early September 1862. On September 2, President Abraham Lincoln placed Major General George B. McClellan in command of the Union soldiers in the nation's capital. "Everywhere, the joy was great," wrote Rutherford B. Hayes, "and was spontaneously and uproariously expressed. It was a happy army again." Nonetheless,

Brigadier General Jacob Cox.
Courtesy of the Library of Congress.

everyone under McClellan's command recognized the importance of the upcoming campaign. "This is our dark hour. We will weather it, I think," said Hayes. The citizens of the Buckeye State who participated in the Maryland Campaign would soon find out if they would, indeed, weather it.[11]

On September 3, 1862, the Ohioans in the Twelfth Corps marched through Washington, D.C., to Tennallytown, kicking off the campaign north of the Potomac River. At midnight on September 4, they received the day's marching orders: "Have your men ready to march at half past eight with two days rations." By September 5, the column had reached Rockville and positioned itself northwest of the capital to protect it from a Confederate thrust in that direction.[12]

The Eighth Ohio in the army's Second Corps joined its Twelfth Corps comrades on the march to Rockville. "We are very dirty and lousy," noted Sergeant Thomas Galwey as the march began. "The shirts we have on our backs now we have worn for about a month." Unfortunately for the Eighth Ohio, their clothing situation would not improve until after the Maryland Campaign ended. "We all scratch alike, generals and privates," Galwey concluded. "The lice have grown to be a perfect torture to us." The regiment, along with the rest of the Second Corps, made it to Rockville by September 7. Despite the regiment's poor appearance, they received a hearty welcome from that town's citizens, "despite the fact that the rebels have been claiming that Maryland was one of their states and only was waiting to be liberated by them."[13]

Major General Ambrose Burnside commanded the army's right wing, which consisted of the First and Ninth Corps. Cox's Kanawha Division formed part of the Ninth Corps. Burnside's initial objective was to march north from Washington, D.C., and reach the National Road, thereby screening Baltimore and protecting that city from the enemy. The Kanawha Division's march began at 7:30 a.m. on September 6. They marched across the Potomac River into Washington and beyond to the city's outskirts. Rutherford Hayes described the day as "very dusty" and "hot." Some men understandably straggled from the ranks, but "all corrected however soon," wrote Hayes at the end of the day.[14]

Cox's division, newly attached to the Army of the Potomac, received its first real impression of the Union's primary army on this march. The Ohioans were not particularly impressed. The Army of the Potomac, said Hayes, "appeared to bad advantage by the side of our troops. Men were lost from their regiments; officers left their commands to rest in the shade, to feed on fruit; thousands were straggling; confusion and disorder everywhere." Colonel George Crook, the commander of the Thirty-Sixth Ohio, attested "that the Kanawha Division compared favorably in discipline and general good conduct with the best troops of the army" while in Maryland. A mild rivalry grew between the Ohioans and the eastern troops of the army that persisted until after the war.[15]

While the Army of the Potomac marched through the border state of Maryland, it was under orders to not pillage from the loyal population. Nevertheless, liberal foraging did occur. One soldier caught hold of a goose as Ninth Corps division commander Brigadier General Isaac Rodman was passing by. Rodman reprimanded the thief and ordered him "sent to the rear, and to be tied fast to the wagon until further orders."[16]

On September 7, Cox's Kanawha Division halted for the day. Immediately on breaking ranks, members of Captain James McMullin's Ohio battery and Hayes' Twenty-Third Ohio took straw from a nearby stack to make their bedding comfortable. As soon as they began dismantling the straw stack, corps commander Major General Jesse Reno arrived on the scene. "You damned black sons of bitches," he yelled to the troops. Reno confronted Hayes over the matter, and the two were able to reach an amicable, if still icy, conclusion to their standoff. As Reno departed the scene, the Twenty-Third Ohio gave their commanding officer a rousing cheer, which gave Reno "great offense." Cox quickly tried to get his Ohioans transferred from Reno's corps "on the ground that General Reno has given such offense to the Ohio troops that they will serve under him with reluctance." How far Cox pressed the matter is unclear, but the Kanawha Division remained under Reno's command until the general's death on September 14.[17]

Overall, the Ohioans in the Army of the Potomac tolerated the march through Maryland. It was a pretty area, and many of the citizens in Maryland were loyal—or at least friendly—to the blue-clad soldiers. Hayes recorded that he never saw his regiment "so happy" as they were when they passed through a central Maryland village and were greeted by the civilians.[18]

By September 12, the van of the Army of the Potomac, the Kanawha Division, was within a day's march of Frederick via the National Road. The Confederate army had vacated Frederick two days prior but had left a rearguard where the National Road crossed the Monocacy River at the Jug Bridge. On nearing the crossing, enemy artillery under the command of cavalryman Brigadier General Wade Hampton opened fire. Federal artillery soon replied as Cox maneuvered his infantry to seize the bridge. Colonel Augustus Moor's brigade moved straight for the bridge, while the Thirtieth Ohio from Colonel Eliakim Scammon's brigade waded through the river upstream from the bridge. The growing federal presence and the fact that Hampton had safely withdrawn all of his command to the west bank of the river convinced the cavalryman that it was time to fall back in the direction of Frederick.[19]

Major General Jesse Reno.
Courtesy of the Library of Congress.

Once over the bridge, Cox formed his division for the advance into Frederick itself. Scammon's brigade deployed in a line of battle on the north side of the National Road, while the Twenty-Eighth and Thirty-Sixth Ohio did the same to the south of it. The Eleventh Ohio marched in the road itself. A battery of Kentucky artillery and a company of cavalry led the way. Once ready, the division advanced "over fences and through cornfields" toward Frederick.[20]

Near the eastern outskirts of the city, a Ninth Corps orderly approached Cox and asked why the command did not move faster. Cox brushed him off, but the man leapfrogged up the column to Colonel Moor and expressed the same feeling to him. Moor took offense to this and dashed ahead with the cavalry company and artillery battery. The battery dropped trail in the road itself. Once in the city, Hampton's cavalryman pounced on Moor and the Chicago Cavalry that served as his escort. Hampton's men attacked with such quickness and shock that it forced the federal cavalry back to the safety of its guns. The gunners yelled for the Chicago Cavalry to clear the road so they could fire into the enemy. Unfortunately, "some of the horses became unmanageable," and one trampled the primed gun's triggerman. As he fell to the ground, he yanked the lanyard and sent a charge of canister downrange, mostly into friendly faces. That blast reportedly killed "eight or nine horses," including that of Moor's staff officer Lieutenant Charles Akoff, who was "badly bruised up by the fall." In the ensuing confusion and melee, Confederate troopers captured Colonel Moor.[21]

From his vantage point behind the guns, Cox ordered the Eleventh Ohio to fix bayonets and advance at the double quick to drive the enemy from the city. The Eleventh Ohio, led by Lieutenant Colonel Augustus Coleman, "formed into divisions of companies" and charged forward to recapture the lost guns. "This movement was executed in admirable style," noted one of the regiment's members. By the time the guns fell into Union hands once more, Hampton's cavalrymen were on their way out the other end of the city.[22]

While gun smoke and its acrid smell still lingered in the streets of Frederick, the liberated city opened its doors and windows to its welcome guests. Reverend William Lyle of the Eleventh Ohio wrote, "It seemed as if the pent-up loyalty of the citizens burst out everywhere and in every form of demonstration." Quickly, "the whole city was arrayed in holiday attire." As the pent-up loyal energy of Frederick's citizens swelled immediately, the Ninth Corps's Ohioans initially sank in exhaustion as they reached the city. "[Men] laid down in the road, saying they couldn't stir again," Lieutenant Colonel Hayes reported. Some were pale, some red as if apoplectic." Frederick's enthusiasm for its liberators summoned the Ohioans' strength. "Half an hour after [they fell out],they were marching erect and proud, hurrahing the ladies!" Citizens "'jumped and down' with happiness." They called the enemy's occupation of their city "the longest week of our lives." Then liberated, they were experiencing "the happiest hour of [their] lives."[23]

It was not all fun and games for Cox's Kanawha Division, though. On seeing an orchard of peach trees on the outskirts of town, one of Samuel Compton's Twelfth Ohio comrades yelled for his company to break ranks and grab the fruit. "The men obeyed with alacrity, and soon, the trees were full of blue coats," Compton recalled. In their haste to grab as many of the peaches as possible, one man lost his grip in a tree and fell out. He landed on a bayonet, "inflicting a severe scalp wound but not serious." Other men found Frederick's delicacies more easily. The Thirtieth Ohio's Edward

Schweitzer wrote, "We was treated to cakes, pies, bread, coffee, apples, peaches." Eventually, the command passed through the throng of excited civilians and camped that night on the city's western boundary.[24]

Following the occupation of Frederick, the rest of the Army of the Potomac awoke early on September 13. Most of it marched along roads that converged in the city. Lieutenant Colonel Franklin Sawyer's Eighth Ohio was up early. After crossing the Monocacy River, a staff officer from army headquarters rode past the men and announced the commanding general's presence. Then, the staff officer said, the men would be allowed to cheer McClellan as he passed by. The men gave McClellan a rousing cheer and did the same for Burnside, who arrived to greet McClellan soon thereafter.[25]

The Twelfth Corps marched in front of the Second Corps that day. As Herbert Smalley of the Seventh Ohio approached Frederick, he scribbled in his diary, "Beautiful country so far through Maryland, and we lived like fighting cocks, potatoes every meal, and peaches to top off with." Smalley's corps remained in that beautiful countryside outside of the city for the rest of the day on September 13.[26]

Smalley's comrades in the Second Corps, however, had the opportunity to pass through the Unionist city. Frederick's citizens turned out once again, just as enthusiastically as they had the day before. In the Eighth Ohio, one soldier said to Lieutenant Colonel Sawyer, "Colonel, we're in God's country again!"[27]

Frederick's thunderous cheers and patriotic displays likely distracted the Union soldiers who were descending on and moving through the city from the booming of cannon on Catoctin Mountain several miles to the west. Just as the rest of the Army of the Potomac stirred on Saturday morning, the federal cavalry rode out of Frederick to seize control of the point where the National Road crossed the mountain. After a long morning of fighting, Alfred Pleasonton's troopers accomplished their objective by early afternoon. By the end of September 13, Pleasonton's cavalrymen sat at the base of Turner's Gap in South Mountain.[28]

Pleasonton's success, coupled with an incredible find by the soldiers of the Twenty-Seventh Indiana on the eastern outskirts of Frederick, made September 13 a particularly good day for the federal troops. Lying in a field outside the city, Sergeant John Bloss noticed an envelope in the grass next to Private Barton Mitchell. At Bloss's urging, Mitchell picked it up and handed it to him. The envelope contained a copy of Special Order No. 191 from the Army of Northern Virginia's headquarters. Mitchell's and Bloss's discovery worked its way up the chain of command and into McClellan's hands.

The "Lost Orders," as they came to be known, confirmed McClellan's intelligence that the Confederate army had marched in several directions from Frederick. Its ultimate intention was to subdue the Union garrisons in the Shenandoah Valley at Martinsburg and Harpers Ferry. McClellan, on verifying the order's authenticity and the fact that the enemy army was still divided, soon ordered his own army to move to strike the divided enemy.[29]

McClellan first ordered Cox's division to move. Thirty-five minutes after dispatching his cavalry chief to verify the information contained in the Lost Orders, another staff officer left McClellan's headquarters at 3:35 p.m., carrying orders for the Kanawha Division. Moving west from Frederick, the Ohioans "made an easy march," Cox recalled, because the friendly cavalry cleared their route of march. They climbed up the slope of Catoctin Mountain. From its peak, the marching men had a view of the Middletown Valley framed by South Mountain in the distance. The valley was "dotted everywhere with the best of farmhouses and residences bearing on its face the marks of fertility and productiveness," wrote Corporal Charles Hay of the Twenty-Third Ohio. Cox and several officers of the division paused at a Washington family home "to look at some relics of the father of the country which were preserved there," which included one of George Washington's uniforms. The officers then remounted their horses and continued the westward march, their "zeal strengthened by closer contact with souvenirs of the great patriot."[30]

By 6:00 p.m., the head of the column made it to the banks of Catoctin Creek, west of Middletown. The division spread out into line of battle on both sides of the creek. They bivouacked amid the remnants of the earlier battle where the National Road crossed the creek between Pleasonton's and Stuart's cavalry. In their retreat, Stuart's men burned the bridge spanning the creek, "but, the water being at a low stage, this vandal act did not hinder [them] in the least."[31]

While the Kanawha Division and the rest of the Ninth Corps marched toward Middletown through the night of September 13, Pleasonton's cavalry skirmished with the enemy at the base of Turner's Gap, a saddle in South Mountain where the National Road crossed the natural barrier. The gap itself stood about seven hundred feet above the valley floor. Pleasonton spent time reconnoitering the area that evening and renewed the effort early in the morning of Sunday, September 14. Artillery support soon arrived to probe the enemy defenses.[32]

To the rear of Pleasonton, Cox's men stirred from their slumber at sunrise. The previous evening, Burnside ordered Cox to support Pleasonton with

Colonel Eliakim Scammon. *Courtesy of the MOLLUS Collection, United States Army Heritage and Education Center, Carlisle, Pennsylvania.*

one of his brigades on Sunday morning. Cox selected Eliakim Scammon's Twelfth, Twenty-Third and Thirtieth Ohio Infantries for the task. They left their camp along Catoctin Creek at 6:00 a.m. Once across the creek, Cox accompanied Scammon's men "to learn how Pleasonton intended to use the troops." There, on the west bank, he surprisingly encountered Colonel Moor, who had recently been paroled by the enemy. Cox rode over to him. After learning Moor's story, the colonel asked, "But where are *you* going?" Cox stated his purpose: to support Pleasonton's reconnaissance of Turner's Gap. "My God! Be careful," Moor exclaimed before remembering that the agreement of his parole prevented him from sharing information about the enemy. Moor quickly turned away and continued walking east, but Cox was on high alert. He immediately ordered Crook's brigade to follow behind Scammon.[33]

As the whole division resumed its march west, Cox rode up and down the column. "It might be a skirmish," he told the regimental commanders, "it might be a battle." He wanted them to be prepared for anything. Cox then asked Corps Commander Reno for additional support before riding off to find Pleasonton. Once together, the two conferred about the strength of Turner's Gap as a defensive position. Three-quarters of a mile south of Turner's Gap, the Old Sharpsburg Road passed over South Mountain through Fox's Gap. Pleasonton suggested that Cox use that avenue of approach to dislodge the enemy from the main pass (Turner's Gap).[34]

Cox agreed with Pleasonton's suggestion. He turned the division off the National Road to the south. "[Our] division filed off to the left through some fields and an orchard" to reach the Old Sharpsburg Road. The men marched slowly due to the terrain and frequently stopped to catch their breath. Near the base of Fox's Gap, Scammon's leading brigade came under artillery fire. To avoid this new threat, he filed his brigade to the left again. The Ohioans began ascending the mountain, utilizing "an old road (used to haul wood)," wrote a member of the brigade. Below the gap, Scammon formed his three regiments into line. Crook's brigade did the same in close support.[35]

Moments before moving, the deployed Ohioans had a chance to take stock of the task ahead of them. "Their position was one of unusual strength," said a soldier in the Twenty-Third Ohio. "[T]heir artillery commanded every path to the mountain, and their infantry were securely posted in the woods and behind stone fence, which latter abound in this country." Crook's brigade did not get the chance to get as good a view of the enemy's position, but the men, no doubt, were aware of the terrain they would have to traverse to seize Fox's Gap.[36]

While waiting and contemplating the fight to come, members of the Eleventh Ohio Infantry received mail from home. "What hasty tearing of envelopes," remembered the regimental chaplain. "Little did the writers of those 'love-notes' think, when writing them, that they would be opened and read amid the booming of artillery and the explosions of shell that made the very earth tremble!" The letters provided the men with comfort "in the hour of peril" and calmed them for the horrors that came next.[37]

It was shortly before 9:00 a.m. by the time Cox's Division completed its deployment. Lieutenant Colonel Hayes's Twenty-Third Ohio held the left of Scammon's brigade, Colonel Hugh Ewing's Thirtieth Ohio occupied the right along the Old Sharpsburg Road and Colonel Carr White's Twelfth Ohio took its position between the two regiments. The brigade fixed bayonets and all was ready for the attack on Brigadier General Samuel Garland's North Carolina brigade, which held Fox's Gap.[38]

Hayes's men on the left moved first. They maneuvered through dense trees south of the farm road, with Company A deployed in front as skirmishers. By Corporal Charles Hay's watch, the Twenty-Third Ohio's skirmishers encountered Garland's men south of the gap at 8:55 a.m. The skirmish fire soon became lively, and Hayes advanced his entire regiment in an inverted formation to meet the opposing Fifth North Carolina. Hayes recorded his regiment "pushed through bushes and rocks over broken ground." The inverted formation and the broken terrain made it difficult for the regiment to keep its line of battle. "I feared confusion," said Hayes, who "exhorted, swore, and threatened" to keep his men in formation. The heavy dose of

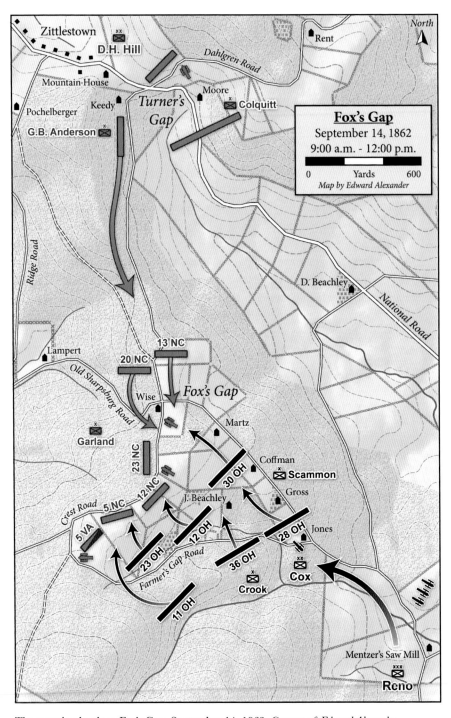

The morning battle at Fox's Gap, September 14, 1862. *Courtesy of Edward Alexander.*

language, threats and encouragement worked. The increased pressure the Ohioans applied to the fight forced the right end of the Fifth North Carolina, partially made up of conscripts experiencing their first combat, to fall back. Hayes did not let the enemy rest once they reformed.[39]

The Fifth North Carolina greeted the Twenty-Third Ohio's second advance with deadly fire. "Found we could not stand it long," Hayes scribbled in his diary, "and ordered an advance." After another stalemate, Hayes ordered a second charge. This advance "was a *real* one," bragged Corporal Hay, who claimed to have crossed bayonets with the enemy. Regardless, Hayes's maneuver worked brilliantly. "With such impetuosity did our troops charge on the enemy that they appeared thunderstruck, scarce knowing what to do or which way to go."[40]

Federal success on the right end of Hayes's line forced Garland to send additional regiments to his stressed flank. One of these regiments advanced forward from the road running along the crest of South Mountain and hunkered down behind "a hedge row and an old stone fence" from which it peppered Hayes's Buckeyes. At a distance of less than one hundred yards, Hayes halted his men behind another stone fence that lined the mountainside. The opposing regiments traded deadly musket fire back and forth. Hayes, looking to break the impasse, ordered yet another charge.[41]

Above the noise of battle, Hayes yelled for his men to drive the enemy back again. No sooner had Hayes risen up to give this command than he "felt a stunning blow and found a musketball had struck [his] left arm just above the elbow." He asked a nearby soldier to turn a handkerchief into a makeshift tourniquet to stop the loss of blood. The makeshift measure barely prolonged the inevitable. Hayes grew weak and laid down behind his line of battle, using his ears to monitor the progress of the action.

Wounded men streamed to the rear, past the prone Hayes. It was likely one of them who told Hayes of a threat to his left flank. He ordered his left company to form perpendicularly to the rest of the regiment's line of battle. The company did so, but it mistakenly prompted the remaining companies to follow suit, and the Twenty-Third Ohio pulled back from its advanced position, leaving Hayes between the opposing lines of battle. Hayes lay exposed to fire from both sides for about fifteen to twenty minutes, he estimated. His survival was an unsure thing at that moment. Near him lay a wounded Confederate soldier. Hayes asked the man, in case he did not survive, to hold onto his personal letters and convey them to his family. The enemy soldier promised to do so. "We were right jolly and friendly," said Hayes. "It was by no means an unpleasant experience."

Left: Lieutenant Colonel Rutherford B. Hayes. *Courtesy of the Rutherford B. Hayes Presidential Library and Museum.*

Right: Second Lieutenant Benjamin W. Jackson. *Courtesy of the Rutherford B. Hayes Presidential Library and Museum.*

Once the fighting quieted—though it did not end—on that end of the line, Hayes called for help. "Hallo, Twenty-Third men, are you going to leave your colonel here for the enemy?" A few brave souls ventured out to do their commander's bidding. The enemy saw their advance and immediately opened fire, "and soon, the battle was raging as hotly as ever." Hayes told his men to seek cover. Despite the growing intensity of the action, Lieutenant Benjamin W. Jackson darted forward and rested Hayes behind a log for cover.[42]

Colonel Carr White's Twelfth Ohio operated on Hayes's right. Through a dense pine wood, the regiment moved into an open pasture field and came under fire. White's men came within close range of the enemy line when they heard "the command to lie down." Private Samuel Compton believed the order came from a private. Regardless, the command "was generally obeyed." Compton remembered, "Never did men lie quicker, even when shot." Those who did not hug the ground and remained standing fell from the withering volley. One of the regiment's early historians claimed to have heard "that entire clouds of lead would momentarily shut out the light in

Flag of the Twelfth Ohio. *Courtesy of the Ohio History Connection.*

their passage." The Confederate volleys were enough to stymie any forward advance made by the Twelfth Ohio.[43]

The pressure on his right forced Garland to weaken his left as he sent units toward the Twenty-Third Ohio's sector of the field. As he was in the process of readjusting his line, Colonel Hugh Ewing's Thirtieth Ohio showed up on the south side of the Old Sharpsburg Road. His skirmishers, under the command of Lieutenant Colonel Theodore Jones, began peppering the North Carolinians. One shot from Ewing's men mortally wounded Garland. Ultimately, the Thirtieth Ohio made little headway as it came under artillery and infantry fire on its front and both flanks.[44]

Scammon sensed the stalemate. To break it, he ordered a section of Captain James McMullin's Ohio Light Artillery, First Battery, from its position along the National Road to Fox's Gap. First Lieutenant George Crome led the two James Rifles to the top of South Mountain in front of

Flag of McMullin's Ohio Battery. *Courtesy of the Ohio History Connection.*

the Twelfth Ohio. The terrain hampered Crome's deployment. Horses were no use on the mountain slope. Crome's gunners manhandled the pieces into position "with difficulty" within forty yards of the enemy. The James Rifles belched forth rounds of double canister while under the harassing enemy fire. As the gunners moved about their work, loading and reloading the pieces, at least three fell wounded. Crome himself jumped in to help load the pieces. He was aiming one of them when a bullet struck him in the breast. The lieutenant died within two hours. His men withdrew and left the guns on the field, though the enemy did not capture them.[45]

Crome's repulse occurred around 11:00 a.m., two hours after the fight began. Unfortunately for the Confederates, any excitement they might have felt at their success did not last long. Colonel George Crook's brigade, formerly that of Augustus Moor, reached the battlefield and added its weight to the Ohioans' offensive. Lieutenant Colonel Augustus Coleman's Eleventh Ohio moved to the division's left to aid the Twenty-Third Ohio in its fight. The Thirty-Sixth Ohio plugged a gap between the Twelfth and Thirtieth

Regiments. Melvin Clarke, a lieutenant colonel, led this regiment. Lastly, Lieutenant Colonel Gottfried Becker's Twenty-Eighth Ohio protected the division's right flank south of the Old Sharpsburg Road.[46]

With the full strength of the division present, Cox ordered his men to charge one more time to seize the gap. "Bayonets were fixed, and at the word, the lines charged forward with loud hurrahs," he wrote. "Our men fell fast, but they kept up their pace," despite the mountainous terrain.[47]

The Twenty-Third Ohio, then led by Major James Comly, surged forward yet again into the Confederate right. "Up and at them!" yelled one of the regiment's officers. "At the word, every man promptly sprang to his feet and, with a deafening shout, rushed forward," wrote a member of Company E. The enemy fired a volley. Comly's men responded before charging forward and initiating a hand-to-hand melee. First Sergeant Thomas Stephens felled three North Carolinians with his bayonet while the regiment's sergeant major, Eugene Reynolds, was killed during the brawl. "'The psalm-singers of the Western Reserve'—as the Twenty-third Ohio was nicknamed—from the hotbed of Abolitionism in the North, had met the boastful champions of wrong and robbery, from the hotbed of oppression and treason in the South; but Freedom's steel, stronger than Slavery's bullets, had signally triumphed!" recalled one fellow Ohioan of the Twenty-Third Regiment's efforts that day.[48]

Augustus Coleman formed his Eleventh Ohio on Comly's left. As the regiment moved into position, its chaplain, William Lyle, recalled the sound of battle that greeted Coleman's men. He said, "The battle was raging fearfully. The indescribable noise of the contending hosts, as they swayed to and fro, like the surging billows of the ocean; the sharp, continuous roll and rattle of musketry; the deep, deafening boom of the artillery, and the crashing, shrieking shell, together with the short, sharp hiss of grape and canister, told a fearful and bloody tale." Once in position, Coleman ordered his men to join the battle. They charged to seize a piece of high ground on the south end of the Confederate line, held that day by the Fifth Virginia Cavalry and two guns under Major John Pelham. Immediately, the

Sergeant Major Eugene Reynolds. *Courtesy of the Rutherford B. Hayes Presidential Library and Museum.*

Ohioans ran into a dense "laurel beings in places almost impenetrable," said one of the regiment's members. Coleman "rapidly reformed the broken ranks," however, and the regiment persuaded the cavalrymen to flee their position.[49]

In the center of Cox's line, Colonel White's Twelfth Ohio advanced, backed up by the Thirty-Sixth Ohio. The Twentieth North Carolina, opposite White's men, slowed the advance but could not stop it. During the advance, a bullet smacked the gun out of Corporal Leonidas Inscho's left hand. He huddled behind the wall that was just vacated by the enemy to examine his wound when he realized a North Carolina captain lay on the other side. "As he came near me," Inscho recalled, "I caught him by

Leonidas Inscho grabs a Confederate soldier and hauls him over a wall. *From Deeds of Valor.*

the collar and told him to surrender." The officer refused and leveled his revolver at Inscho. Moments before he squeezed the trigger, Inscho grabbed hold of it and was able to direct the shot straight into the air. Inscho wrestled him to the ground and over the stone wall, disarming the officer in the meantime. With one prisoner and the revolver in his hand, Inscho implored the captain's men to surrender. Four of the five soldiers did so. The fifth took a cheap shot at the corporal but missed before darting into the woods. Inscho's heroics earned him the Medal of Honor.[50]

While Inscho performed his heroic act, his regiment continued after the foe. "The enemy," said Private Compton, "fled like deer." In their haste and excitement at having finally sent the enemy running, White's Ohioans continued over the mountain's crest and three hundred yards down its western slope. During their drive over the mountain, Division Commander Cox sent White a note to "hang on," to which White replied, "General, we are driving them and have no wish to stop as long as a rebel lives." Eventually, the terrain and hostile artillery fire stopped White's advance.[51]

The charges by Cox's left and center regiments cleared Fox's Gap of most of Garland's brigade. Only the Thirteenth North Carolina and Captain James W. Bondurant's Jeff Davis Artillery remained. The Thirtieth Ohio attacked the North Carolinians' front. Soon, the other successful Ohio

Joseph Ash Joel completed this image of the Twelfth Ohio's and Twenty-Third Ohio's charge at Fox's Gap. Joel was a member of the Twenty-Third Ohio and was wounded in the Battle of South Mountain. *Courtesy of the Library of Congress.*

regiments began to press their flank, including the Twelfth Ohio, which got back underway after suffering under Bondurant's guns. White's restarted regiment nearly succeeded in capturing the guns near the Wise garden but ultimately came up empty-handed. However, the pressure they provided alongside the Thirtieth and Thirty-Sixth Ohio Regiments forced the last of Garland's men from the gap.[52]

This final fight for Fox's Gap was a confused action as far as formations were concerned. "So dense was the laurel that the troops were obliged, in many places, to move in single file, and our lines consequently became much broken," wrote Captain Solomon Teverbaugh of the Eleventh Ohio. "However, the men moved forward, and when separated from their commands, each one acted for himself and struck where he saw his blows were most needed." Individual actions like Inscho's were not exclusive, though these other actions did not all warrant medals.[53]

During the action on the federal left that involved the Eleventh Ohio, some of the regiment's members became separated and fell into enemy hands. One of the captors did not rush the prisoners to the rear immediately, claiming, "It was no use to be in a hurry, for they would have a lot more in a moment." In the regiment's final advance, Lieutenant Colonel Coleman,

Joseph Ash Joel. *Courtesy of the Rutherford B. Hayes Presidential Library and Museum.*

mounted on horseback, outpaced his men and soon found himself among the enemy. "Seeing he was in a bad snap," Coleman drew his sword and yelled to the captives of his regiment, "What are you doing there?" They replied that they were prisoners. "Prisoners," Coleman yelled, "get your arms immediately!" Coleman spurred his horse into the cluster of enemy soldiers and told them, "If they didn't surrender immediately, he'd cut them to pieces." Fooled by Coleman's bravado, twenty-three enemy soldiers surrendered to him, one of whom capitulated along with the flag he carried. One refused to and fired two quick shots at Coleman, neither of which hit him. The offender "fell, pierced by seven bullets."[54]

After three hours of fighting to secure Fox's Gap, the Kanawha Division finally succeeded. The fight was a desperate one. Garland's command lost 44 men, 168 were wounded and close to 200 were captured. In total, the brigade lost nearly 40 percent of its pre-battle strength. Cox's division lost 324 men in total. Most of those casualties came from Scammon's brigade, specifically the Twenty-Third Ohio. The division was far from wrecked, however.[55]

There was still plenty of daylight left for Cox to finish the task of turning the enemy's position at Turner's Gap to the north. However, several factors made this more difficult than it initially seemed. Though the Kanawha Division then possessed Fox's Gap, the battlefield did not fall silent. Cox's right flank, which he described as "too much in the air," fell under the fire of several enemy artillery batteries. Cox also learned from the host of Confederate prisoners that was then in his hands that D.H. Hill's entire division—five brigades—stood in Cox's path to Turner's Gap. "Longstreet was said to be in near support," Cox added. The division also lost about 10 percent of its strength in the morning's desperate fight. With less than three thousand men, Cox did not feel he could drive Hill's and Longstreet's troops with the strength he had. He decided to wait for the rest of the Ninth Corps to arrive. While they held the crest, the clock ticked past noon, and Cox's men sought any cover they could from the enemy artillery shells, which "cut long furrows in the sod with a noise like the cutting of a melon rind."[56]

Beginning around 2:00 p.m., the other divisions of the Ninth Corps began to arrive in Fox's Gap. First came Brigadier General Orlando Willcox's division. Brigadier General Samuel Sturgis's division moved into position two hours later. Before dusk, the corps's last division, led by Brigadier General Isaac Rodman, reached the battlefield. Corps Commander Jesse Reno remained along the National Road with Burnside and McClellan, leaving Cox as the corps's senior officer present on the field, responsible for the afternoon's fight. His Kanawha Division played a less prominent role than it had in the morning, but Cox gave orders and positioned the corps for its next fight. "During all this time, there was sharp fighting all along the front," Cox wrote, "the struggle being on the part of the Confederates to drive back our center and left, where we held the highest summits of the mountain, and on our part to push forward our right so as to gain the one elevation they still held on our side of the National Road at the Mountain House" in Turner's Gap. "Good progress was made" by the federals in this fight, Cox reported, but nightfall found the corps still facing the enemy ensconced in Turner's Gap.[57]

Before the sun fully set on September 14, Reno reached his corps's frontline position to kickstart a renewed advance from Fox's Gap to Turner's Gap. When the corps's commander reached the front and saw the Kanawha Division's success, he exclaimed to Scammon and Ewing, "Gentlemen, you have kept your brag," in reference to the run-in Reno had with his Ohio troops a few days prior. Then, in the waning daylight, Reno rode to the front, where he fell, mortally wounded, leaving Cox in command of the corps. Cox admitted in his later years that after the morning fight, "it was time to rest" his division. Then it was the corps's turn to catch its breath from a day of marching and fighting.[58]

The men of the corps, especially those of the Kanawha Division, appreciated Cox's prudence with his men's energy. Aside from fighting up a mountain, some of the Ohioans went through the day's struggle without water. "No one can imagine the torment of going through a day's battle without water," said Private Compton. "After fighting all day, we were glad to rest on our arms at night," wrote another. The Kanawha Division's soldiers tried to get whatever sleep they could among the dead and wounded of the battlefield. "The regiment bivouacked in line of battle—one rank guarding while the other slept or, rather, rested, as the night was too chilly for sleep— the knapsacks, blankets, &c., having been left in the rear," recalled one of the Eleventh Ohio's soldiers.[59]

Alexander Wight, one of the Twenty-Third Ohio's musicians detailed to the medical corps, described his fellow nurses and surgeons as "completely" tired out. Unfortunately for them, it had been a trying day. "Just think of the band, only fourteen strong, carrying off all the wounded and taking care of them," he told his brother nine days later. Throughout the day, Wight helped carry eighty-eight wounded men nearly one mile to the rear. Nightfall did not stop his work. They "had to stick to it and then sit up all night."[60]

One of the men Wight assisted to the rear was Lieutenant Colonel Hayes. "I went to him and offered to help him, but he told me there was plenty worse off than him," Wight said. Hayes remained there a brief time before the medical corps moved him farther from the front lines. He found refuge at the home of Jacob Rudy on the west end of Middletown.[61]

Joseph Webb, a surgeon of the Twenty-Third Ohio and Hayes's brother-in-law, selected the brick home. The Rudys—Jacob, his wife and their two sons and five daughters—graciously accepted the officer into their home, even though one of their own sons was already sick. Mrs. Rudy quickly prepared the bedroom next to her sick son for Hayes's use. Webb's brother James arrived to aid Hayes. On September 23, Lucy Hayes, the lieutenant colonel's wife, reached Middletown. "Lucy is making me very happy and comfortable," Hayes informed his mother.[62]

Lucy Hayes helped cheer the wounded of her husband's regiment, too. She found them "lounging wherever there was a shady place, some with heads bandaged, some with arms in slings, others limping badly." After attending to her husband, Lucy brought grapes and other fresh foods to the wounded soldiers, "rebels and Union men alike," recalled Mrs. Rudy. She read to the wounded and grew to have "a great many favorites, but she was attentive to all and admired by everyone."[63]

The wounded Ohioans of South Mountain and Antietam received other visitors in the battles' aftermath. Governor David Tod sent physicians from the Buckeye State to Maryland to offer any assistance they could. Ohio's surgeon general Gustav Weber was surprised to find Hayes in Middletown. He examined Hayes's wounded arm. According to a postwar recollection, Hayes had asked for his arm to be amputated shortly before Weber's arrival. Both Webbs decided to save Hayes's limb, a decision that was

The Rudy home still stands along Main Street in Middletown. *Courtesy of Kevin Pawlak.*

Surgeon Joseph Webb. *Courtesy of the Rutherford B. Hayes Presidential Library and Museum.*

confirmed by Weber. As the Ohio delegation departed from Hayes's presence, the wounded officer told them, "Tell Governor Tod that I'll be on hand again shortly."[64]

Hayes's stay at the Rudy home lasted three weeks. Hayes and his wife left for Ohio on October 5, 1862. The bond between the Hayeses and the Rudys did not end in October 1862. "We fell in love with him directly," said Mrs. Rudy. Hayes returned to Middletown to visit the Rudy family in 1864. Kate Rudy, one of the daughters, visited Lucy Hayes in Columbus in 1868. On Election Day in 1876, Jacob Rudy, who "was very unwell," still voted for Hayes, who won election as the nineteenth president of the United States. The elderly Rudy died around Christmas 1876. One of Rudy's sons wrote to Hayes, announcing his father's death. Hayes's reply reached Middletown "within a week." "It expressed the utmost sympathy for us all and roverted kindly to the time when he was disabled and had a home with us."[65]

While the Kanawha Division battled for Fox's Gap on September 14, the other Ohioans in the Army of the Potomac marched toward the scene of battle. Members of the Fifth, Seventh and Sixty-Sixth Ohio Regiments comprised a column of Union infantry marching through Frederick for the third consecutive day. The enthusiasm of Frederick's citizens apparently did not let up from their previous encounters with the Army of the Potomac. "At nearly every window were displayed the Stars and Stripes by ladies fair, as they bid us welcome and Godspeed," remembered Captain Frederick Seymour of the Seventh Ohio. "On through town we passed, with lighter hearts and footsteps, all feeling that we left friends behind us, and not, as in Virginia, lurking, secret foes to shoot down our pickets."[66]

The soldiers of the Twelfth Corps caught the Union-loving sentiments of Frederick's populace. One soldier began singing "John Brown's Body." A band picked up the tune, and soon, recalled Maryland Campaign veteran and historian Ezra Carman, "it [was] taken up, regiment after regiment, [was] carried from the leading brigade through the whole division, from one division to another, until the grand chorus, swelling from thousands of voices, [filled] the whole air and [produced] an effect beyond the comprehension of those who know not, from experience, the capability, power and richness of a man's voice when a man's heart is in it."[67]

George B. Ray was one of the Fifth Ohio's musicians who likely lent his musical talents to the stirring scene. Buoyed by the patriotic fervor for their cause, Ray and his comrades continued west from Frederick with the echo of artillery from South Mountain growing louder with each passing step. As the Twelfth Corps descended Catoctin Mountain, the National Road became packed with artillery and wagons, forcing the infantry to march through the fields alongside it. After dark, the Twelfth Corps finally came to rest in the streets of Middletown. Before long, commanders shook their men awake. By midnight, the corps had halted near Bolivar, east of Turner's Gap. It was a tortuous march that, by Ray's count, covered sixteen miles.[68]

The Eighth Ohio and its comrades in the Second Corps took a different route over Catoctin Mountain to alleviate the traffic on the National Road. They traveled via the Shookstown Road, north of the National Road. A citizen guide led the column over the mountain using what Thomas Galwey described as "a bridle path. It is hard work for us and even harder for our artillery," he noted. From the top of the mountain, the men spied the smoke rising from the fighting at Fox's and Turner's Gaps. However, they noted they could not hear it. Galwey ascribed this to "some atmospheric condition." His commander, Lieutenant Colonel Franklin Sawyer, claimed that "the tramp of our twenty-five thousand men, the rattle of our artillery along the stony roads, and the hum of subdued tones of voice among our troops completely shut out any sound from beyond." Regardless, everyone noted that the visible battle lacked its usual audible accompaniment.[69]

By nightfall, the Second Corps, likewise, had reached Bolivar. "Soon, we came upon the dead and wounded, ambulances and stretchers," wrote Sawyer, "and finally halted at the foot of the mountain among the dead and amid the scenes of the day's carnage." September 14 was a long day for all the Ohioans in the Army of the Potomac, and there was still more work to be done. After their day of marching and fighting, they tried to get what rest they could, though some found that to be more difficult than others. Lieutenant Colonel Sawyer said, "There was but little chance for sleep. The men were crowded together on the ground where the battle raged, the ground was filthy and damp, the ambulances were rattling by all night, and the stretcher-carriers busily hunting for the dead and wounded." That grisly process continued throughout the night, a stark reminder of the trials yet to come.[70]

2

"It is Impossible at This Time to Speak of Individual Bravery"

Tyndale's Buckeyes

On Monday the 15th, we were early on the march," Captain Frederick Seymour of the Seventh Ohio wrote from his regiment's bivouac within sight of South Mountain. The Army of the Potomac's Twelfth Corps was in motion toward the mountain gaps. The corps, commanded by Major General Joseph K. Mansfield, included the Seventh Ohio Volunteer Infantry, as well as the Fifth, Twenty-Ninth, Sixty-Sixth Ohio and Twenty-Eighth Pennsylvania Regiments. These units comprised Lieutenant Colonel Hector Tyndale's First Brigade of Brigadier General George Sears Greene's Second Division. The morning was typical for the men in the ranks. Although they rose early to begin their march, the accordion nature of a column on the move and the collision of the army's unofficial motto of "hurry up and wait" meant that the brigade really did not get underway until 9:00 a.m.—and only at a slow rate. Not long into their slow-paced march that morning, these Buckeyes reached the battlefield of the previous day. As they did so, Private Herbert Smalley of the Seventh Ohio "saw about fifty secesh prisoners and a couple of blacksmith wagons captured with them. Ambulances passing continually, loaded with wounded." Yet again, the column came to a grinding halt. Smalley and two others "went to see the battleground of the day before. Ground strewn with dead secesh in every direction. Our dead all buried. One man leaning against a tree, stone dead. Trees all cut up with balls and shell."[71]

The column slowly started back up again. Smalley, his two friends and others who took the time to explore the ghastly site of the previous day's fight fell back into the ranks. Finally, the brigade made it through Turner's Gap at South Mountain and reached the small town of Boonsboro. To Private Smalley, it seemed as though the aftermath of the Battle of South Mountain followed them as they reached the town. He remembered, "Every house full of the killed and wounded." While in Boonsboro, a number of men recalled seeing and cheering on their beloved army commander, Major General George B. McClellan. Captain Seymour wrote of the moment several weeks after the conclusion of the campaign. "As we moved on in pursuit of the fleeing foe, our men in good spirits,

Lieutenant Colonel Hector Tyndale. *From* A Memoir of Hector Tyndale.

wrought up by the presence of our great Chieftain, Gen. McClellan, as he rode through the ranks, it was pleasant to see the countenances of our men light up with joy, as they rent the air with cheer after cheer, which was gratefully acknowledged by the gallant general." Private Smalley agreed, noting that the men around him "cheered him lustily."[72]

Despite another pause in their march, there was still daylight left and several more miles ahead of the Ohioans in Tyndale's brigade. "After marching 'till dark this night, the 15th, we bivouaced [*sic*] for the night," recorded Captain Seymour. A soldier in the Seventh Ohio who signed his name "Julius," believed the regiment and, thus, the brigade "halted for the night about three miles from Boonsboro." The usual chores began for the men not long after they halted, gathering firewood, cooking dinner and coffee and bedding down for the night. As they laid down, beginning to ponder what the next day would hold for them, many heard "very heavy cannonading over to [their] right."[73]

"On the morning of the 16th, we were aroused from our bed on the ground and received the order to march," Seymour recorded. As most men of the brigade shuffled, sleepy-eyed, into the column, others sought to fill their haversacks before the march. Private Smalley recorded, "On waking, found myself close to an apple orchard. Went over the fence and 'confiscated' about a pack. Knew they would make me sick but could not resist the temptation to 'scoff' about a dozen." With General Greene's division formed, "in quick time, [they] were on the move to support the batteries, but after an hour's artillery dueling, the rebels fell back across Antietam Creek." Musician

George B. Ray recorded in his journal that those orders to move came at approximately 10:00 a.m., with further instructions to load their weapons as they did so. The order raced down the line "to 'load at will,' and then 'prime,' we were somewhat surprised at this, as it was our custom not to prime 'till we saw something to shoot at," Smalley noted. Musician Ray estimated the brigade only moved a mile to support a federal battery then heavily engaged. Marching in rear of the guns, the Buckeyes of Tyndale's brigade were then "halted in 'close column of attack by companies.'"[74]

While waiting to go into action or further support the batteries to their front, another order reached the brigade. It read, in part, "to stack arms and make ourselves as comfortable as possible." By the time the brigade's men had stacked their arms, the "sun [had] came out terribly hot, and [there was] nothing bigger than a thistle for shade," recorded Smalley. Despite the rising temperatures from a warming sun, "Our men set about making coffee, the soldier's only solace, after which, choosing the softest place on the ground, sought that rest and sleep so much needed by our nearly exhausted men," Captain Seymour observed. The hours ticked by, and still, no further orders had come to the Ohio regiments. Dinnertime approached. Those lying about once again went through the task of making something to eat and boiling their favorite ration, coffee. One Seventh Ohioan said, "Made a cup of coffee and went in 'snucks' with a Co K. man who had some shingles of which my 'chuck-bay' was innocent. Went over to the 23d regt.'s train and invested half a dollar in shingles and pork, which I divided with the co. Pitched my tent and lay down with a full paunch and a clear conscience." Others in the brigade did the same thing, many believing there would be no further work for them until the next day.[75]

Writer "Julius" of the Seventh Ohio believed this to be the case. "We had lain down in line of battle expecting to remain until the morrow, the tattoo had sounded, and an impressive silence had settled upon the bivouac, broken only by the tread of the alarm guard, as he slowly paced his beat, and the occasional passage of an orderly conveying some order to be executed in the coming day," he wrote. Captain Seymour agreed. With "night setting in, without further orders, we prepared to pass the night." "Not long were we to rest. Our ears were soon assailed with—a 'Attention, first brigade!' And we were soon in line and moving around to the right," Julius recalled. Private Smalley recorded the time the orders broke their sleep. "Slept well 'till about 10, when the accursed call to fall in was sounded, and we were obliged to cut short our dreams and strike our little tents as hastily as possible," he wrote. Men like William Baxter in the Sixty-Sixth believed it to be a little later.

"Lay[ing] all day until 10 ½ O'C P.M. then march[ing] all night," he said. It took the brigade a full hour to fall in and start its march. Musician Ray recorded that the time the brigade finally started moving was approximately 11:00 p.m. It was a "slow and tedious" march, "as all night marches are." The night march was grueling on the men, further exhausting the rank and file. Herbert Smalley recorded the route the brigade took to its new position and the effect it had on the men in the column. "Marched down the pike to Cadysville [Keedysville], where we turned to the left and crossed two stone bridges in succession. Passed a large barn and was sorely tempted to fall out and sleep 'till morning." However, he "kept a stiff upper lip…and stuck it out. Very disagreeable marching. Go a half dozen rods and then halt 'till we all got asleep and then fall in and go as much farther. Kept this up 'till three in the morning, when we, at last, halted."[76]

Finally, at 3:00 a.m., on the morning of September 17, 1862, Tyndale's brigade came to a standstill. Exhausted, cold and damp with sweat, the men quickly fell out, found a place to lie down and collapsed into a deep slumber. Silence fell over the men. Only "an occasional shot or volley in an adjoining piece of woods reminded us of the close proximity of the enemy; nevertheless, the rest of the night was passed quietly enough by us." Not everyone in the ranks found that quiet quickly or easily. Private Smalley said, "Tried to get to sleep but could not on account of a very noisy argument in Co C. as to which was the more bulky, wet sand or dry. Stood it as long as I could and then got up and gave them a short lecture on the value and necessity of sleep, after which they dried up." The Buckeyes did not sleep for very long. "[S]carcely had the first tints of daylight broke upon the eastern horizon, when the roar of the artillery and musketry startled the slumbering soldier, and the order came to 'fall in,'" recalled Captain Seymour. "With aching heads and benumbed limbs, they quickly obeyed the order and were on the march." The Battle of Antietam had begun.[77]

For many in Tyndale's brigade and in the Ohio regiments thereof, they had less than two hours of sleep. It proved to be a long day. After laying down sometime at 3:00 a.m., just two hours later, "at 5 a.m. we were called up, the men took their places in line without waiting for breakfast, moved forward about a quarter of a mile then halted and got breakfast," musician Ray recorded. Captain Seymour in the Seventh Ohio was thankful for the halt and the opportunity to make coffee. "Fires were soon kindled, and the most of our men were able to get their coffee," Seymour wrote. Yet, not everyone was able to brew coffee, especially those who were slow risers in the morning. As the men in the ranks found firewood and got their coffee prepared, the

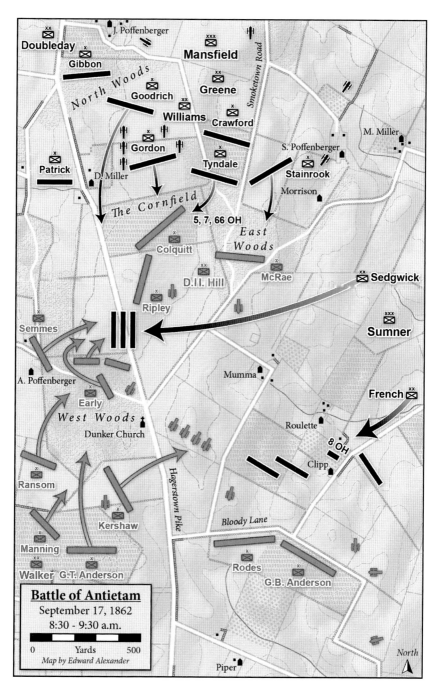

Tyndale's brigade clears the cornfield, and the Eighth Ohio attacks the Bloody Lane.
Courtesy of Edward Alexander.

early sounds of battle rippled across the air not far from their position. While the men sipped their coffee slowly from their tin cups, the tangible evidence of the fight drifted through their lines. Smalley witnessed "wounded men passing to the rear in great numbers." With the crescendo of musketry and artillery fire, orders filtered down from the Twelfth Corps's headquarters to the divisions, brigades and regiments that comprised the corps. For the Ohioans in Tyndale's brigade, those orders were received sometime around 6:00 a.m. Officers, including Seymour, were responsible for getting the men ready to move out. According to the orders he and the other Ohio officers had received, the "men were formed in column of division [and]…in this order, we moved on in solid column 'till we reached a point of the woods where the enemy were in heavy force and were holding our men in check."[78]

Tyndale's brigade, along with the rest of Greene's division, arrived at the front in a "mist [that] was so dense that we could not see but a short distance." The scenes and sounds of battle soon engulfed their senses. The brigade wasted no time in deploying into line of battle. One Ohioan believed the time was 8:00 a.m. when the brigade deployed, while other records place it earlier, sometime around 7:00 a.m. The arrival of the corps did not occur without notice by the enemy. Colonel Evander Law, in command of a brigade of Confederate troops that was then on the field, wrote in his official report that he was able to see "a powerful federal force (ten times our number) of fresh troops" move onto the battlefield. Certainly, Law witnessed the arrival and deployment of the two divisions of the corps and possibly the three brigades of Greene's division that brought up the corps's rear, with Tyndale's brigade bringing up the division's rear. As they pushed southward to extend the line of the First Corps, their movements while in column made Greene's division appear as a massive fresh force. It belied their true numbers, as many Confederate accounts describe the massive size of the federal reinforcements at this time during the battle. It was not long before new orders raced down through the division to deploy into line of battle and prepare to go into action.[79]

"'Forward,' shouted General Mansfield, and forward we went in columns of divisions as cool and regular as in a drill," remembered Julius of the Seventh Ohio. The brigade, following Mansfield's command, "marched into the woods where the rebels were masked behind a fence." Tyndale's brigade surged forward, yet as they did so, they struggled to see the opposing line of battle. Some in the Ohio ranks later claimed that the Confederate line of battle laid on the ground and, coupled with their dirty uniforms, made it "difficult to see where they were, but we soon learned, for the leaden hail came thick and fast." At the same time, during the advance, Lieutenant Colonel Eugene Powell of the Sixty-Sixth Ohio and Major Orrin Crane of the Seventh Ohio went back and forth on who exactly was in their front. Crane continually posited that the troops opposite their front were friendly, while Powell strongly disagreed. The conversation became moot. The two right flank regiments of the brigade front had come upon the dangling flank of the Sixth Georgia Infantry. Powell's Sixty-Sixth Regiment unleashed a deadly volley. The Fifth and Seventh Regiments quickly followed with their own, officially bringing the Ohioans into the fight.[00]

Major Orrin Crane. *Courtesy of the Library of Congress.*

Both lines then erupted into sheets of flame. Tyndale's brigade found the Confederate line in the northern end of the East Woods on the northern end of the battlefield. This fight was short but intense. Captain Seymour estimated the exchange between the two lines lasted only twenty minutes before "we drove them from their shelter and put them to flight." With the Confederate line of battle falling back, Julius wrote, "Gen. Green [*sic*] shouted—'Charge!' With a yell of triumph, we started with leveled bayonets, and, terror stricken, the rebels fled. Like hounds after the frightened deer, we pursued them for fully three-fourths of a mile, killing, wounding and taking prisoners at every rod." A private in the Seventh Ohio witnessed a similar scene from his position in the line.

> *When we came up, our men were falling back, but our heavy and well-directed volleys soon turned the tables on the Greybacks, and after firing 15 or 20 rounds at them, we got them on the run and followed them up through a cornfield where their dead lay in great heaps. We chased them some half a mile, firing as we went, and then one of our batteries came up on the run and poured in a terrible round of grape and canister. This entirely broke their ranks, and they fell back in a perfect panic.*

The Sixth Georgia practically ceased to exist. The Ohioans performed well in the first moments of the battle, a great feat considering the three Buckeye regiments numbered less than 450 men in total. The retreat of the Confederates from the East Woods and D.R. Miller's cornfield, scenes

Post Antietam flag of the Sixty-Sixth Ohio. *Courtesy of the Ohio History Connection.*

of intense fighting and high casualty rates, left an indescribable horror behind. It was worse than anything they had seen during their service thus far. Reflecting back on the moment, Captain Seymour said, "The carnage of that bloody field was terrible beyond all description. No language can describe, nor pen ever picture it." Lieutenant Colonel Eugene Powell "was amazed, when we reached the ground [where] their line stood, at the terrible execution that we had done. The dead were piled up so thick that we could hardly pass without stepping on them."[81]

With the Confederates in full retreat toward their fallback line west of the Hagerstown Pike, the field was clear for the Ohioans of Tyndale's brigade to continue to press forward. With Mansfield mortally wounded and out of the fight, Brigadier General Alpheus Williams took over command of the corps. Williams believed he could use both of his divisions to attack from opposite directions, sweeping the Confederate brigades south of the cornfield and into a trap that they would not be able to escape; essentially, it was a tactical pincer movement. Greene's new orders from Williams were to deploy his brigades into line to the east of the Joseph Poffenberger farm lane, march southward and swing his left flank toward the Mumma farm complex, sweeping up Confederate units as he went. Instead of a due south movement, in accordance to Greene's instructions from Williams, the brigade shifted to a southwesterly advance and pushed toward the Dunker Church, a patch of high ground just opposite it, east of the Pike, and the disorganized Confederate line went racing for the protection of the main line and the West Woods. Tyndale's men pursued the fleeing Confederates for almost an hour, "giving them no time to rally their confused and disordered ranks," Captain Seymour recalled. The brigade finally came to a halt near a piece of ground known today as the Dunker Church Plateau. While the men in the ranks stopped to catch their breath, the musketry along the brigade line sputtered out. Seymour believed "each man had from 60 to 70 rounds at the commencement of the fight. So, it may safely be inferred that there was some shooting done." "'Men, have you plenty of ammunition?' 'No, only ten rounds left,'" was the phrase heard up and down the line in the ranks of the Seventh Ohio. Orderlies were sent to the rear immediately to find Greene, apprise him of the situation and have him assist in getting more ammunition to the front. Seymour estimated that it took only half an hour before ammunition arrived. Once the men were ready to reenter the fight, the line of battle was dressed, shifted slightly to the right and marched forward to the crest of the Dunker Church Plateau.[82]

Between the time of their deployment on the rise of ground just east of the church and pike—some time before 9:00 a.m.—and 9:30 a.m., combat swirled around Tyndale's brigade. They were able to see bodies of organized Confederate troops move off toward their north and beyond their flank. The Ohioans witnessed the arrival of Major General John Sedgwick's Second Corps division on the battlefield and their drive westward into combat in the West Woods. To their immediate right and front, they watched fellow units from Michigan, New York and Pennsylvania be driven out of their toehold just across the pike and flee toward the rear. Yet for Tyndale's men, there had been a break in the action after their initial success earlier that morning. Then, with Sedgwick's division in bad shape, their line was starting to crack, Second Corps commander Major General Edwin Sumner sent for assistance from the Twelfth Corps and General Williams. The two closest units at hand, the Thirteenth New Jersey and Second Massachusetts, were immediately ordered toward the Dunker Church. Even though these units moved at a quick-step, the hole created in the line between Tyndale's

Monument dedicated to the Fifth, Seventh and Sixty-Sixth Ohio Infantry Regiments.
Courtesy of the Library of Congress.

right flank and Sedgwick's division created a tempting opportunity. The Third South Carolina set out to capitalize on it. Racing northeast across the Hagerstown Pike and past the Ohioans right and rear, they were soon stopped cold. A solid line of federal artillery opened on them, as well as those survivors who had just retreated to the safety of those guns. It was a close call for Tyndale's exposed flank, but he soon had other challenges ahead of him, including the approach of Brigadier General Joseph Kershaw's brigade.

Events continued to transpire around the Ohioans that did not bring them into the fold. Off to their right, the Thirteenth New Jersey had finally arrived, but as the musician Ray of the Fifth Regiment described, "They soon turned and ran, just as the Rebels were driving our boys back." Meanwhile, Kershaw's Confederate brigade shifted more toward the southeast during their push across the pike, striking Tyndale's sister brigade on his left flank, which was under the command of Colonel Henry Stainrook. Captain Seymour witnessed the destruction of the Second and Seventh South Carolina off to his left. He recorded that the South Carolinians were "holding their men as best they could and fighting with the desperation of fiends, seemed determined to perish rather than yield." Kershaw's units pulled back under the withering fire. Not long after the attack of the South Carolinians to their left front, Tyndale and Stainrook's men saw another brigade driving on their position. Under the command of Colonel Vannoy Manning, the mixed brigade included regiments from North Carolina, Virginia and Arkansas. "Julius" of the Seventh Ohio did not so much see the new threat advancing towards his position but, rather, heard it. "A yell in the distance denoted an advance of their infantry," he remembered. Tyndale's brigade opened fire on them. They were accurate and deadly. Major Orrin Crane of the Seventh Ohio wrote in his official report of the destruction his regiment and the brigade inflicted on Manning's advancing line. When Manning's brigade was "within a short range, our troops were quickly thrown forward to the top of the hill, where we poured into their advancing columns volley after volley. So terrific was the fire of our men that the enemy fell like grass before the mower," he reported to his superiors. "[S]o deadly was the fire that the enemy retreated in great disorder, they not being able to rally their retreating forces."[83]

Prior to this action, the brigade had been pulled back off the crest of the plateau in order to provide shelter and protection to the men while not being directly engaged. Private Robert S. Bower of the Seventh Ohio remembered this minute detail from the battle, writing, "Our brigade was lying at the brow of a hill when a brigade of the enemy advanced on us. The front rank of our co. [H] was deployed at the top of the hill, and fired on them until they were within ten rods. We then fell into line, and the brigade moved up and fired volley after volley into them, until they skedaddled in true Southern style." As the Fifth, Seventh and Sixty-Sixth Ohio Regiments and the Twenty-Eighth Pennsylvania pursued the retreating remnants of Manning's line, Private Smalley remembered the brigade's "tremendous cheers fairly drowned the noise of the firing." Tyndale's and Stainrooks brigades charged forward, across the pike, capturing the Dunker Church and hundreds of prisoners. They did not stop until they had advanced about two hundred yards into the West Woods. Major Crane described what happened next in his official report. "We charged them in a heavy piece of woods, driving them out of it, capturing a large number of prisoners…and made terrible havoc in their ranks, covering the ground with the slain, many of them officers."[84]

Now far from any federal support, their right flank dangling unsecured and unanchored, Greene's line was in a precarious situation. The situation was even more grim for the Fifth and Seventh Ohio Regiments. After successfully breaking the Confederate advance, accomplishing everything they had during their pursuit and creating a new line deep in the Confederate position, these two units were low on—if not out of—ammunition. They could only hold on for so long before a counterattack would be made to dislodge them. General Greene immediately sent for support. The Thirteenth New Jersey and the Purnell Legion answered the request. Musician Ray of the Fifth Ohio believed his unit and its sister regiment, the Seventh Ohio, "held our ground until 2 p.m., when another brigade took our place." Not sure of the exact time, writer Julius of the Seventh Ohio believed they "held the woods for nearly two hours, when our ammunition being out, we fell back, the Thirteenth New Jersey taking our place." Major Crane agreed with the length of time they held their new position, writing in his official report, "We gained the woods and held our position for two hours. We were then ordered to retire and be relived [sic] by other troops under the command of General Smith." Private Smalley estimated the total time they were engaged and described the reason for falling back when he wrote, "After six or seven hours of as hard fighting as this war can boast, being short of ammunition, we fell back a short distance to obtain a fresh supply." Finally, the Fifth and Seventh Ohio Regiments were relieved. They recrossed the Hagerstown Pike and took up positions on either side of Powell's Sixty-Sixth Ohio and in support of Captain John Tompkins's First Rhode Island Light Artillery, Battery A. Julius recalled seeing them deploy and get into the fight. "The gallant Eighth Rhode Island Battery [Tompkins's Battery] comes up in splendid style, our ranks opened right and left for them," he wrote. Then "the exhausted battery of howitzers [Monroe's Battery] wheeling out of line. The parrotts were unlimbered, and, 'Shell, five second fuse!' called for, and they opened in glorious style." The brigade continued to hold this plateau and was later rejoined by Stainrook's brigade. Ultimately, however, the battle shifted away from their front, farther to the south and the Confederate right flank. The Buckeyes had fought for over six hours, sustained numerous casualties and continuously ran low on ammunition. It was time to pull them from the front line.[85]

"Gen. Green [*sic*] ordered us back to rest our men…as our troops had been constantly under fire of the hottest kind since six in the morning. It was after one P.M., and our men were glad to get a chance to rest, for they were nearly exhausted," wrote Captain Seymour. "The day was very warm and the work terrible." As the Buckeyes pulled back, many of them made sure to take their souvenirs from the field with them. Sergeant Isaac Jones of the Seventh Ohio said, "A good many of our boys have trophies picked up on the field. Atwater of company C took a lieutenant colonel prisoner and has his sword and belt for his trouble."[86]

John P. Murphy had an even bigger trophy that he brought off the field. Born in 1844 in Killarney, Ireland, he had a challenging childhood. Not only had his family come to America and faced the stigmas associated with being a poor Irish Catholic during the mid-nineteenth century, the family moved around several times. When John was ten, both of his parents died. There was no longer time for schooling, as John was forced to make his way in the world. He had hardly entered the workforce as an apprentice before the outbreak of the war. At the age of seventeen, John Murphy enlisted in the Fifth Ohio Infantry. He was only eighteen years old at the time of the Battle of Antietam. During the fighting around the Dunker Church, Murphy captured the flag of the Thirteenth Alabama Infantry. Passed up the chain of command, the captured flag was not returned to the state of Alabama until a government order forced the return of captured flags to Southern states in 1905. John P. Murphy was presented with the Medal of Honor for his actions at Antietam four years later, on September 11, 1866.[87]

For the first time that day, since their initial engagement with Confederate infantry, the Ohioans had a chance to take stock of what their charges cost their respective regiments. Scores of their wounded streamed rearward during the day. Although some of the wounded survived the side effects of their treatment and recovered from their wounds, many did not. Corporal Edward W. Goodsell, Private David Everett and Private Allison Coe, all from

This owl on the Fifth, Seventh and Sixty-Sixth Ohio Infantry monument represents the Wide-Awakes. *Courtesy of the Library of Congress.*

the Seventh Ohio, succumbed to their wounds at the Smoketown Hospital over the next several days and weeks. The same fate befell Private George Howard of the Fifth Ohio and Privates John J. Kohler and Casper Mowser of the Sixty-Sixth Ohio Infantry, all dying from their wounds at Smoketown. Other wounded Buckeyes were taken to private homes, then acting as field hospitals, and even evacuated to Frederick. While the Ohio units got their wounded off the field and to places of treatment and care, the sobering reality of the dead left behind on the field sank in. Scores of Buckeyes had been killed during the battle. In the Fifth Ohio, Privates William Spellman, John M. Miller, Lorenzo Kendall and Jacob Gutlzer were among the many on the casualty list. Privates George O. Sperick, Henry Bacon and Eldridge F. Meacham, all of the Seventh Ohio, were placed on the list of those killed in action. Over the coming hours and days, the casualty list of the Ohio regiments continued to grow as more information became available. These names represent only a small fraction of Buckeye casualties sustained in Tyndale's brigade during the September 17, 1862 battle. Each name, however, can be found on a government headstone in Antietam National Cemetery today.

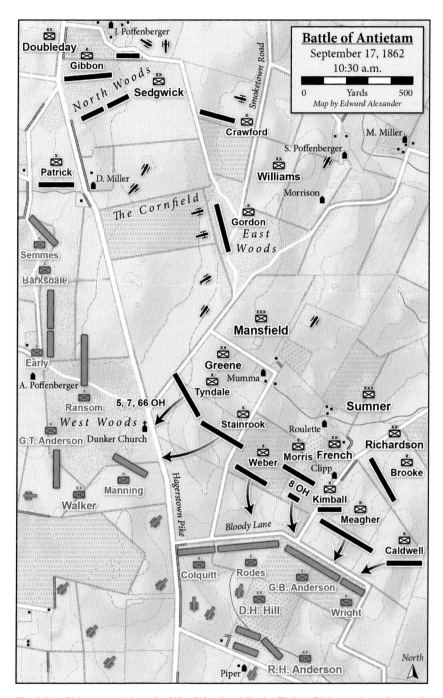

Tyndale's Ohioans push into the West Woods, while the Eighth Ohio continues its attack against the Bloody Lane. *Courtesy of Edward Alexander.*

Now that they had been moved to the rear from their position near the plateau, the battle was essentially over for Tyndale's brigade. Captain Seymour noted some exchanges between the two picket lines that evening, which kept "up their dueling, and many a soldier that night went out to duty who returned no more." Throughout their experience on September 17, the three Ohio regiments in the brigade performed well, even more so considering the small number of them in the ranks. Private Robert S. Bower recognized the performance of not only the regiments and brigade but also of the division. Speaking of Greene's division, Bower said, "And, if I say it, they did go in, for we never stopped after we had started [at] the grey coats, 'till we had driven them nearly a mile. They rallied several times and came on us by brigades, but a few well-directed volleys and a charge would make them run, and then what a beautiful chance it gave us to shoot at them. I tell you we of the Seventh took good aims with our Springfields." At the brigade level, Private Smalley praised brigade commander Tyndale for his actions during the battle, and the men showed their support in return. "During a lull in the fight," Tyndale, Smalley wrote, "rode up, and taking off his hat, cried out, 'Boys, you have fought nobly; and by the Great God who looks down upon us, you shall have your reward! What the Ohio and Pennsylvania boys can't do, nobody can!' He was answered by deafening cheers." Sergeant Isaac Jones praised both his brigade commander, Tyndale, and division commander Greene. "Lieutenant Colonel Tindal [*sic*]…who commanded the brigade, did bully," the Ohio sergeant noted, "and General Green[e], whom we all hissed and hooted whenever he passed, acted so bravely that when we halted and sent back for ammunition, we really got up three cheers for him. He thinks the Ohio boys are hard to beat in a fight."[88]

At the regimental level, Private Smalley boasted of his commanding officer's performance, writing that Maj. Crane "cannot be too highly praised for his coolness and bravery during the fight." The commanding officers also made sure to praise the work performed by the men in the ranks. Crane wrote not only of his own men, but he also praised the entire brigade for their actions that day. "It is impossible, at this time, to speak of individual bravery," he said in his official report, "but I can say, without flattery, that all, both officers and men of the different regiments of the brigade, nobly stood by their colors and did their duty well on that eventful day." John Collins, in his official report of the Fifth Ohio's service during the battle, succinctly spoke for all the Ohio regiments in the brigade at Antietam when he wrote, "It is no flattery to say that officers and men did their duty bravely during the whole of the six hours' fire to which they were subjected."[89]

3

"One of the Hardest Fought Battles of the War"

The Eighth Ohio Infantry at Antietam

We are up at dawn on Monday the 15th," wrote Thomas Francis Galwey of the Eighth Ohio Volunteer Infantry. Although they had missed the fighting for the gaps through South Mountain the previous day, they did not escape the horrific reality the battle left in its wake. The regiment's march on September 15 began at 6:00 a.m., a difficult proposition, as there had been "but little chance for sleep" the night before. Lieutenant Colonel Franklin Sawyer, commander of the Eighth Ohio during the Maryland Campaign, wrote that the regiment camped on the battlefield proper on the night of September 14 and into the morning of September 15. "The men were crowded together on the ground where the battle had raged, the ground was filthy and damp, the ambulances were rattling by all night and the stretcher-carriers busily hunting for the dead and wounded," recalled Sawyer. Before continuing their march from the previous days, Sawyer made sure that his men had cleaned their weapons and had sixty rounds of ammunition issued to the regiment. Not sure what the coming hours—or even days—would bring, Sawyer wanted to make sure his men had functioning guns and plenty of ammunition in case battle was imminent.[90]

Finally, the day's marching orders filtered down from Second Corps headquarters, arriving to Sawyer through Third Division commander Brigadier General William French and First Brigade commander Brigadier General Nathan Kimball. It was not until after Major General Israel Richardson's division had moved through the gap at approximately 10:00 a.m. that the second and third divisions of the corps finally began their march. As the men moved in full daylight through the gap, the sights around them only grew more ghastly. It was not long before they saw "Confederate dead at every step," Thomas Galwey remembered. "I saw two poor dead bodies under a projecting rock," recalled Galwey. "They had, most likely, crawled under there when wounded and then died. They lay as though they had been in conversation just before their death."[91]

Much of the march on September 15, 1862, reflected the daily lives of soldiers on campaign. The accordion nature of the column, the long delays, halts and pauses before a short movement forward. It was a grueling, maddening pace for the men in the ranks. But the veterans of the Eighth Ohio were well accustomed to the U.S. Army's unwritten policy of "hurry up and wait." These men had answered President Lincoln's initial call for seventy-five thousand men in the spring of 1861, hailing from such cities and towns as Tiffin, Cleveland, Bucyrus, Norwalk, Sandusky, Fremont and Elyria. The men in the ranks of the Eighth Ohio Volunteer Infantry also represented a wide swath of Ohio's counties, coming from Seneca, Crawford, Huron, Erie, Sandusky, Lorain and Medina Counties. Not long after the regiment's organization and arrival at Camp Dennison, Ohio, it re-enlisted for three years, as its initial three month service had come to an end. Just one month later, the Eighth Ohio joined the army in West Virginia, where it campaigned until July 1862. From there, it joined the Army of the Potomac at Harrison's Landing and remained with that army for the remainder of its service. Before joining the aforementioned army,

Lieutenant Colonel Franklin Sawyer. *Courtesy of the Library of Congress.*

these Buckeyes had seen combat at Romney, Winchester and Front Royal. Combat-tested, as the men marched toward the battle and their destinies at Antietam, they were under the capable leadership of Lieutenant Colonel Franklin Sawyer.

Franklin Sawyer was thirty-six years old when he entered the federal service as a captain of Company D, Eighth Ohio Volunteer Infantry. Born in Auburn Center, Ohio, in July 1825, he had attended Norwalk Seminary and Granville College and was admitted to the bar during the Mexican-American War in 1847. Just three years later, Sawyer's career was on a rapid rise, a sign of things to come in his military service. In 1850, he was elected as the county prosecutor of Huron County and became well established in the community before the war. Then, serving as the captain of Company D, Sawyer continued to rise through the ranks. By July 1861, he was promoted to major, and four months later, lieutenant colonel. When Colonel Samuel Sprigg Caroll of the Eighth Ohio was promoted to brigade-level command, Sawyer took over the command of the regiment, a position he held until mustering out.[92]

Only two hours into the march, the column was halted once again. "Jack Sheppard, my messmate," wrote Galwey, went "foraging in one direction and I in another. He return[ed] with a fat duck and I with potatoes. So, we have dinner. Forward again." After a day on the march, with some light skirmishing along the way, Sawyer, Galwey and the others of the Eighth Ohio "moved, after dark, to beyond Keedysville." Galwey and his messmates were excited for the opportunity to rest, get some sleep, and make the soldier's most favorite ration. "At last, after our coffee, we settle ourselves for sleep," Galwey wrote of the evening. As the regiment further settled in, Lieutenant Colonel Sawyer noted that the regiment "again [laid] on our arms, the divisions being masked behind a considerable ridge, which hid us from the enemy."[93]

With daylight growing, the position the Eighth Ohio had settled into the evening prior became more clear. Sergeant Thomas M. Ebright, in a letter written a week after the battle and later published in the *Holmes County Farmer* on October 9, noted that the surrounding terrain "was a long a plateau, variously interspersed with slight depressions that present excellent cover for troops in the shape of cornfields, stone-walls, small forests, one or two lanes or country roads, washed deep by the rains of other years, served admirably as rifle pits." As the lines of battle took shape that day, Ebright wrote that it "was some five miles long, a portion of Antietam creek, a stream not easily fordable and crossed by substantial stone bridges." Sergeant Galwey expanded on Ebright's description of the position of the Eighth Ohio on the morning of September 16. "[W]e had been formed in mass by brigades," Galwey noted. "The position of the corps was along the reverse slope of a low ridge that ran parallel to Antietam Creek....The right of our brigade touches the turnpike connecting Keedysville with Sharpsburg."[94]

The position of the Eighth Ohio and that of their brigade were tactically selected "in support of our batteries that had opened up an argument with the Confederate artillery, which was posted on the other side of the creek and just back of Sharpsburg," remembered Azor H. Nickerson thirty-one years after the battle. Nickerson continued to lament the hatred of the infantry being placed in support of a battery, particularly on September 16. "Supporting batteries is always irksome," Nickerson recalled, "and when the enemy has found your range and occasionally drops a ten- or twenty-pound shell in your ranks, it is both disagreeable and dangerous." The sporadic artillery fire between the opposing batteries, continued throughout the day, often with stray shots and overshots landing among the Eighth Ohio's position. Lieutenant Colonel Sawyer made sure that his men kept a low profile, out of sight of Confederate gunners who were still trading shots with several federal batteries near their position. The day progressed in this manner until a continuous, rolling thunder grew into a cacophony of chaos and noise. A large artillery duel had opened after a day filled with measured fire. Sawyer and several others cautiously moved up to the federal artillery position, where they watched "the red glare of flame along the rebel line for more than a mile, the answering volumes of fire from our batteries, the bright streams of light along the track of the shell, and the livid clouds of smoke as the shell burst in the air, constituted a spectacle brilliant beyond comparison." While some curious onlookers in the Eighth Ohio crawled forward to watch the duel, others moved farther rearward behind their position.[95]

First Lieutenant Azor Nickerson of Company I recalled his servant, "a colored boy…who rejoiced in the name of Joe White…came very near turning white in person as in name," as more and more Confederate rounds landed in the Eighth Ohio's position. The lieutenant recalled that Joe's expression and movements displayed a sense of fear and uncomfortableness with each new shell landing near them. As one shell screamed in, a soldier in camp "started to run across the open space that separated the battery from the infantry," striking him and "taking off one of his feet above the ankle. He was going so fast that he took two or three steps on the mangled stump before he fell." The scene made Joe even more pale. The rounds continued to fall among the regiment. One shell landed near the color guard, which had only recently stacked its muskets, placed the colors on the stack and sipped on some freshly made coffee. Lieutenant Nickerson, who observed the shell's impact, believed that it was from a twenty-pound cannon, based on the size of the round and the destruction from its impact. The shell had "plunged into the ground in the middle of the group. The dust flew in a cloud as the men apparently jumped to their feet." Not all of them survived. The dust settled from the shell's impact, and Nickerson "saw that one man, the color corporal named Farmer, had not arisen."[96]

Corporal William Whitman Farmer had enlisted in Company D of the Eighth Ohio on June 4, 1861. He was an older enlistee, signing his enlistment papers at the age of thirty-five, and although he was originally from New York, he had long since become an adopted Buckeye. Witnessing Farmer not getting up, Nickerson ran to him and noticed that the shell had not exploded and was still lying nearby. When he got closer to Farmer, eventually kneeling by him and gently raising him to examine his wounds, he noticed that the shell "had torn away the man's whole side; he was dead almost as soon as I reached him." Thomas Galwey also witnessed the death of Farmer and how the veterans around had become so hardened to the horrors of war. Galwey wrote, "A piece of the shell literally cut him in two. But we cooked our breakfast and chatted as usual. Some of the men gambled." This tragedy made Azor Nickerson's servant, Joe, "look whiter than ever….This was too much for 'Joe.'" The young servant ran to a pile of rails that had been stacked for firewood later that evening, seeking cover from the storm of shells. It was not long before yet another Confederate shell struck the Eighth Ohio's position. This one hit the ground hard, glancing upward, and took off the top of the pile of rails, sending them everywhere. It brought "Joe to his feet, as white a looking negro as was ever seen. Finding that he was not hurt, he started at full speed to the rear, and I saw him no more that night."[97]

At some point during the artillery engagement, the commander of the Army of the Potomac, Major General George B. McClellan, arrived in the vicinity of the Eighth Ohio and the line of federal guns near their position. Although he was a native of Philadelphia, McClellan had an established, firm relationship with the Buckeye State before the war and during its earliest days. In 1860, he became the president of the Ohio and Mississippi Railroad, and in April 1861, he was commissioned as a major general and placed in command of Ohio's militia. Two weeks later, McClellan re-entered federal service as the commander of the Department of the Ohio. An early war regiment, the boys of the Eighth Ohio quickly recognized General Mclellan as he "passed along the face of the ridge. His gallant bearing compelled our admiration. We gave him a rousing cheer." Their hearty cheer had the negative effect of causing the enemy batteries to focus on the large cohort of mounted officers.[98]

September 16, 1862, finally drew to a close. The Eighth Ohio only suffered the loss of a few men. Although the darkness brought an end to the day's artillery engagements, the ripple of musketry was heard off to the Eighth Ohio's front. Soon, that action sputtered out, and "at night, we lay down to sleep on the same ground where we had been all day. Everything became terrifically quiet," wrote Sergeant Galwey. Lieutenant Colonel Sawyer, still wanting to ensure his regiment was ready at a moment's notice, had the men lay on their arms that evening. In later years, following the war, both Sawyer and Galwey, two of the most prolific writers for the Eighth Ohio during that era, reflected on those few hours before the sun broke on September 17, 1862. Galwey recalled the "quiet that precedes a great battle has something of the terrible in it. Everyone knows that there must be fought a bloody battle tomorrow and all are therefore anxious to save their strength for the contest." Sawyer also remarked on the silence in the camp that evening. In the regimental history, Sawyer wrote of the men's "quiet slumber—many, alas!, for the last time," and of the "clear and beautiful, still and awfully solemn," night—all thinking of the coming battle. Their slumber did not last long, however. Sawyer received orders to call roll at 3:00 a.m. and to have the regiment in line, ready to move at a moment's notice, following roll call. For the men of the Eighth Ohio, it would be a long day.[99]

Sergeant Galwey wrote wryly that the men were up early on Wednesday, September 17, for the "day's merry-making." As dawn's early light broke across the horizon, two things quickly became evident: the battle at Antietam had begun, and it was perfect meteorological conditions for a fight. "With daylight came the roar of artillery and the din of battle in Hooker's front," wrote commander Sawyer. As the sound of battle grew with each passing moment, the sun rose higher on the horizon. "The weather is all that could be desired…clear and hot," wrote one soldier of the Eighth Ohio. With more light streaking across the battlefield northwest of the Eighth Ohio's bivouac, orders streamed down the chain of command for more reinforcements to be sent to the growing front.[100]

Galwey recalled that the men barely had time to eat their breakfasts before the regiment received orders to take arms and march, "crossing the turnpike, march[ing] nearly in the direction which Hooker's men took last night." Men were "moving in every direction," he continued. One day after the battle, Lieutenant Colonel Sawyer submitted his official report of the part the Eighth Ohio played. In it, he described the route of their advance to their first position after leaving their bivouac from the night before. "We left our bivouac on the east side of the creek…moving in our proper position in the line, forded Antietam Creek and deployed in line of battle on the hills," he reported. What opened before the regiment's eyes was nothing short of jarring.[101]

Arriving on the battlefield between 8:45 and 9:15 a.m. (Galwey recorded it was 8:00 a.m.), the destruction and death of the early morning fight between Major General Joseph Hooker's corps and the Confederate left flank were seen everywhere. Galwey astutely realized Hooker's corps was already *hors de combat*. The Twelfth Corps had also been in the thick of combat. Major

General John Sedgwick's division, which crossed Antietam Creek ahead of French's, deployed into line of battle and raced westward, toward the growing fight around the Dunker Church and the West Woods. Their arrival had extended the Union army's line on its left flank toward the southeast. Meanwhile, French's division halted in the East Woods at approximately 9:15 a.m. It was not long before orders arrived for French to move on Sedgwick's left and advance with a two-divisional front into the West Woods. Thus, French looked to deploy his three lines of battle "adjacent to and contiguous with Sedgwick." Sedgwick, however, did not wait for French, and his rapid push toward the growing fight across the Hagerstown Pike did not allow French to realize this plan. French deployed his division into a three-brigade front and pushed them almost due south toward the exposed left flank of Brigadier General George Sears Greene's division of the Twelfth Corps. French's three stacked brigade lines consisted of Brigadier General Max Weber's brigade in the front, Colonel Dwight Morris's brigade in the middle and Brigadier General Nathan Kimball's brigade in the rear, with the Eighth Ohio as the second regiment in the brigade line from the right flank.[102]

Their route of march took them past the burning Mumma farm buildings and toward the Roulette farm. As the first brigade in French's line, Weber's men had made it past the Roulette farm buildings when they came under fire from the Eighth South Carolina. By 9:30 a.m., Weber's brigade had cleared the southern end of the Roulette property and begun their attack on the center of the Confederate line at the Sunken Road. The federals' first attack wavered almost immediately from the withering volleys of Alabama and North Carolinian soldiers sheltered in the stout defensive position of the sunken lane. French's second brigade in line, Morris's men, soon came to Weber's aide but to little avail. Meanwhile, Kimball's brigade was held in reserve, with the Eighth Ohio just north of the Roulette orchard and around the farm's outbuildings. First Lieutenant Nickerson of Company I remembered that the regiment, along with the brigade, was:

> *Halted in the orchard while Morris' brigade was advanced to the crest of the line of little hills, which lay distinctly in front of and parallel with a deep ravine, and a cornfield beyond. As soon as they reached the crest of these rises of ground, they were met by a tremendous volley from the enemy posted in the ravine and cornfield. They wavered for a few minutes, then breaking, came back at a Bull Run pace, threatening to overrun everything that stood in their way. Our lines that stood fast and by shouts of "cowards" and threats to "charge bayonets" on them if they did not halt, they were checked.[103]*

Flag of the Eighth Ohio that the regiment carried at Antietam. *Courtesy of the Ohio History Connection.*

Following these initial failed attempts by federal soldiers to pierce the Confederate's defensive position in the Sunken Road, French's division traded offensive tactics to a defensive posture. It was a sound judgment. Moments later, the brigades occupying the Sunken Road moved to counterattack. Disjointed at best, the effort was quickly turned back.

While Brigadier General Robert Rodes's Alabamians moved against the right flank of French's line, the general received orders to continue to drive his attack. General Sedgwick's attack in the West Woods was under immense pressure, and Second Corps commander Major General Edwin Sumner needed that pressure to be relieved. General French immediately ordered his reserve brigade, Kimball's men, to charge forward. A veteran of the battle and early historian of Antietam, Ezra Carman relayed the next moments. "The men were lying down, and Kimball called them to attention. 'Boys, we are going in now to lick the rebels, and we will stay with them all day if necessary,'" he wrote. Kimball ordered his men to take off their knapsacks and pile them under the trees in the orchard. After fixing bayonets, "the entire line, starting at the double-quick, moved steadily and magnificently forward, over the open plain, under a heavy fire of shell and in the face of a sheet of musketry." Captain Benjamin F. Ogle of Company A recounted the moment more contemporaneously than Carman's history did. The captain recalled, "Our line was ordered to charge, which was successfully done, driving the enemy over a hill and into a lane, so washed by the rains as to form a natural breastwork, in which they crowded and were reinforced by fresh troops who poured into us a most deadly fire."[104]

As Kimball's brigade swept forward, numerous men from the division's two other brigades were carried with them. Many were younger, less experienced regiments that had been thrown into the first line of French's assault toward the center of the Confederate position. As this latest effort came within musket range of the Alabamians and North Carolinians in the Sunken Road, "again, the enemy poured forth a murderous fire….The air seemed hissing hot with rifle balls. Crashing through our ranks would come terrible discharges of grape and canister, while the bursting of heavy shells from a battery directly in our front would create a juvenile earthquake about the head." The exchange between the two lines intensified, with Confederate artillery also harassing the ranks of the Eighth Ohio. Captain Daniel Lewis of Company C remembered, "The air appeared to be filled with shot and shell, and the crack of musketry was perfectly deafening, and a constant and dense column of smoke ascended from the lines." Meanwhile, the Confederate line in the Sunken Road strengthened their position, preparing for an assault that was sure to come. Lieutenant Sawyer watched as Confederates from Alabama and North Carolina piled up fence rails and even their dead comrades in front of their lines. The two opposing lines continued to blaze away at each other. Ezra Carman noted that the boys from Ohio and Indiana were "firing at the heads and shoulders of such of the enemy as exposed themselves in the sunken road and at others who were firing from the cornfield beyond."[105]

Lieutenant A.H. Nickerson from Elyria, Ohio, was in command of Company I during the battle. Wounded in the shoulder, he returned home for care and recovery just five days after the battle. A report of his experiences, those of the men under his command, and others from the Eighth Ohio began to appear in many newspapers later that day, September 22—and for the next week. After taking their position south of the Roulette farm by bayonet, Lieutenant Nickerson recalled from his home in Ohio, "The enemy were strongly posted in front of a hill, drawn up in two lines of battle….The Ohio…boys stood fully exposed to the enemy." Nickerson was later quoted in the *Fremont Journal*, "[We were] exposed to a murderous fire, but not an Ohio man flinched." There, supporting Kimball's brigade, were the remnants of French's other two brigades, fighting "side by side with us gallantly."[106]

Kimball's brigade sustained significant casualties in a matter of minutes. The Confederate brigades of Robert Rodes's and George B. Anderson's well-directed rifle and musketry fire to the Eighth's front and the Confederate artillery fire into their right flank made their continued attack almost untenable. One of the earliest casualties the Eighth Ohio experienced during the charge was Lieutenant Horace Harper Bill. Born on April 4, 1842, in Sandusky, Ohio, he enlisted in Company K on June 25, 1861, at the age of nineteen. In a post-battle letter to Bill's father, Earl, Colonel Sawyer said of his death, "[He] fell early in the engagement, pierced with three balls—one in the head; one in the body, passing through his sword belt; and one in the leg. He was not conscious after this, but life was not entirely extinct until near night." The loss was a devastating blow to the regiment. "His uniform, good conduct, kind heart, cheerful spirits, and constant attention to his duties won the affections of all." Colonel Sawyer, in his closing and perhaps speaking for all the losses the regiment sustained that day, wrote, "Thus early in life has passed away one of our brave and promising youth." Lieutenant Bill was not the only casualty the Eighth Ohio suffered that day.[107]

Thomas Galwey also remembered the immense casualties the Eighth Ohio sustained at this stage of the fight. "[O]ur men are falling by the hundreds," he recalled. "Our brave orderly sergeant, Fairchild, sticks doggedly to his position, his face streaming blood. Jack Sheppard, my old mess-mate…drops. He is shot in a dozen places." Galwey continued to write about those falling around him. "Lieutenant Delaney is shot in the bowels…. Lieutenant Lantry…[had] the top of his head…taken off by a shell. Our company is narrowing more and more. There is but a small

Lieutenant Horace Harper Bill, Courtesy of the Sandusky Library Archives Research Center.

group of us left. Fairchild is bleeding; Champion falls, mortally wounded; Jim Gallagher's head is badly grazed." William Kinney, also of Company B, "wanted to get Lt. Lantry's body home, but they won't let us take his body off the field," he wrote to the *Cleveland Plain Dealer*. General Kimball, while riding by the Eighth Ohio's position during this time, muttered, "God save my poor boys!"[108]

The orders from General Kimball—and, thus, to Colonel Sawyer—for the Eighth Ohio to charge arrived after 9:30 a.m. Over the course of the next hour, Kimball's brigade and the Eighth Ohio Infantry, as well as the remnants of French's other two brigades, continued to trade shots with the well-positioned Confederate soldiers in the lane. French's division needed reinforcements to continue the fight. It was not long into the Eighth Ohio's ordeal that Major General Israel B. Richardson's division arrived on French's unsecured left flank. Leading Richardson's division were Brigadier General John C. Caldwell's brigade and Brigadier General Thomas F. Meagher's famed Irish Brigade. By this time, according to Colonel Sawyer, "Nearly half the officers and men of the Eighth were killed and wounded, and the loss in the balance of the brigade was equally appalling." The Eighth Ohio had more problems than just high casualties; their effectiveness to continue the fight waned with each passing moment. "The men complained that their guns were foul or their ammunition exhausted," reported Sawyer. "The ground was covered with arms along the field, and the men were ordered to change their pieces for these, and the officers, at once, went to picking up and distributing ammunition, and in this way, and by cutting the cartridge boxes from the dead, a good supply was soon obtained."[109]

General Richardson wasted no time in getting his brigades on line as soon as they were on the field. On their deployment to the Roulette property, Meagher immediately carried out his orders. The Irishman pushed his brigade forward, and once they were within range of the Confederate position, they were to fire and charge. Although this attack had numerous failures, it relieved the pressure on French's battered regiments, including the Buckeyes. But Kimball's brigade and French's division were not the only units on the field that were receiving much needed reinforcements. Confederate brigades under the command of Brigadier Generals Ambrose Wright and Roger Pryor and Colonels Carnot Posey, Alfred Cumming and William Parham reinforced the Confederate position.

The Eighth Ohio continued to fight on, sustaining casualties at an alarming rate. In Company A, Privates William P. Richardson and David Zongker were killed in action. One of the musicians in Company C,

Frederick E. Nichols, was killed; he was only twenty-two years old at the time of his death. Officers were also falling at an alarming rate. Sergeant John Briggs in Company D had fallen, instantly killed. He was twenty-five years old. Another officer, Sergeant Jonas Baser of Company F, died of his wounds on October 6 at a field hospital in Frederick, Maryland. Charles Boughton, a corporal in Company H, fell during the Eighth Ohio's fight with a mortal wound, succumbing just four days later. In Company E, nineteen-year-old Franklin Trube was killed in action, while Private John M. Conner was mortally wounded, dying at a field hospital a week later. Men in Companies F and G were also being hit. Privates John Fields and William Palmerton of Company F were both killed, as were John Keesan and Orville Cole, both of Company G. Also mortally wounded was Darwin D. Newell, aged twenty-two. Newell, a private in Company K, died of his wounds in a Frederick hospital eight days later. Azor Nickerson was also hit at this time. He remembered feeling "the sharp jab of the bullet, a blur about the eyes, and the warm blood running down my right side as that arm fell helpless." The bullet had struck him in the shoulder joint, traveling down the arm and exciting near the elbow. Nickerson headed toward the rear and found a field hospital.[110]

Around 12:00 p.m., a New York regiment from Caldwell's brigade had advanced onto the flank of the Sunken Road position. Like dominoes, Confederate regiments from the right flank pulled back or retreated, the dominoes continuing to fall toward the center of the line. Confederate General Robert Rodes ordered his right flank regiment, the Sixth Alabama, to refuse their line in order to secure what was left of that flank. Confused orders at the regimental level led Rodes's brigade to pull out and retreat. It was impossible to stop the rout, despite Major General D.H. Hill, who was in command of the division, grabbing a musket and leading small bands of men back toward the lane. As more federal units pushed into the Sunken Road and beyond it, Confederate general James Longstreet was able to organize a small body of Confederate infantry and several pieces of artillery to attack General Kimball's right flank in an effort to slow the federal pursuit beyond the lane and to buy time for reinforcements to arrive. "All at once, a new danger opened upon us," wrote Sawyer in regards to Longstreet's attack. "Sedgwick had been completely driven from our right, and suddenly, grape-shot and other missiles struck us from the right and rear."[111]

As the two small Confederate units approached Kimball's right flank, Kimball saw the dire situation his brigade was in and ordered the Eighth Ohio and Fourteenth Indiana to change front into a plowed field just south

The Eighth Ohio's monument stands in the Bloody Lane. *Courtesy of the Library of Congress.*

of the Roulette farm buildings. The two units, low on ammunition after being on the firing line for nearly two hours, fired what they had into the Confederate attackers. Despite this fire, the Eighth Ohio received as much as it doled out. Colonel Sawyer wrote, "This fire, for a moment, was excessively galling." The Confederate attack pushed on. The Ohioans, as the enemy drew closer, noticed "an officer mounted on a white charger." The Eighth Ohio unleashed a volley toward their target. The "gallant leader with his horse fell, the line reeled, broke and fled."[112] The volley, combined with the fire of the other regiments by the side of the Ohioians, was enough to stop the attack. During this exchange, Sergeant A.D. West fell. Lieutenant Elijah T. Hayden wrote from near the battlefield to Reverend C.C. West of Sergeant West's final moments. The letter was later published in the *Elyria Independent Democrat*. At the time the orders were given to change front, Hayden relayed that "most of our men did not have a single cartridge to put in their guns. It was at this time and place your nephew fell, shot through the heart with a minnie ball." Hoping to provide comfort, Hayden relayed of West:

> *During the whole engagement…*[he] *evinced the most unexampled bravery and courage, constantly in the front, cheering on the men…during the 17 months that he has been associated with us, he did most cheerfully discharge all the duties of a solder* [sic]*; we feel that we have not only lost a true and brave soldier but a most able and efficient officer. He had risen from true merit from a private to 1st sergeant, and had he lived, he would have received a commision of which he was truly worth.*

Albert West was twenty years old.[113]

The Eighth Ohio was still not done for the day. Another potential threat required the left wing of the unit to change front yet again. The rest of the Eighth Ohio, however, headed toward the Sunken Lane, where the fighting between the two lines had sputtered out. Captain Wells W. Miller of Company H was ordered to take command of the Confederate prisoners who had been captured in the Sunken Road and escort them to the rear. Colonel Sawyer later reported that, in total, Captain Miller escorted between two and three hundred prisoners rearward, many of whom were wounded. While the Buckeyes gathered prisoners and took stock of the scene the Bloody Lane presented, some sought out momentos of the fight. Colonel Charles Courtenay Tew, the regimental commander of the Second North Carolina Infantry, had received a grievous head wound at some point during the battle. While the federal troops continued to gather wounded Confederates from the lane and send them rearward, one Ohio soldier found Tew "apparently unconscious, the blood streaming from a wound in the head, with his sword held by both hands across his knees." This story, which was relayed to Captain Matthew Manly of Company D, Second North Carolina, on the Antietam battlefield 35 years after the battle by a soldier of the Eighth Ohio, revealed, "A federal soldier attempted to take the sword from him, but he drew it toward his body with the last of his remaining strength, and then, his grasp relaxed, and he fell forward, dead." Manly later published this exchange in the history of his unit in 1901. At the time, the whereabouts of Tew's sword were unknown. "The sword was given by the soldier to the colonel of his regiment, who, unfortunately, is no longer living, and the sword, having passed into other hands, cannot be recovered." In 2015, the sword was given by the Thirty-Third Signal Regiment of Ottawa, Canada, to The Citadel on the Antietam battlefield at the approximate location where Tew had died. Before the sword was returned, research was completed by the Thirty-Third Signal Regiment to track its odyssey to the United States' northern neighbors. They were able to identify a "Captain Reid" as the soldier who took the sword from Tew on September 17. A quick look at the roster of the Eighth Ohio reveals two "Captain Reids" at the time of the battle, each named John and serving in Company D. From the battlefield at Antietam, to Ohio, New York, Canada, back to Antietam, and finally to The Citadel, Colonel Tew's sword was no longer missing after 153 years.[114]

Colonel Charles Tew's sword briefly returned to the Bloody Lane in 2015 as it was transferred to Tew's alma mater, the Citadel. *Courtesy of Kevin Pawlak.*

Between 1:00 and 2:00 p.m., the Eighth Ohio was finally relieved. The Buckeyes, along with the rest of Kimball's brigade, withdrew and reformed around the Roulette outbuildings, barn and house. Although they were resupplied, each man refilling his cartridge box and told to be ready to re-enter the fight should they be needed, the Eighth Ohio's role in the Battle of Antietam was over.

When Colonel Sawyer wrote the regimental history in 1881, he remembered the number of casualties the regiment had sustained as "fearful." In all, he counted 162 officers and men having been killed or wounded, a number he believed to be approximately half of what he took onto the battlefield that day. Private John A. Chichester of Company B wrote on September 18 that the battle of the previous day had been "one of the hardest fought battles of the war" for both the Eighth Ohio and the Army of the Potomac. Chichester believed that "the brigade fought splendidly" and said, "We have not disgraced Cleveland." Thomas Francis Galwey, also of Company B, agreed, writing, "The brigade had achieved undying renown. It had taken and held one of the most difficult and important positions on the field and had maintained an unwavering line during the carnage of four hours' battle. Gen. Sumner pronounced it the 'Gibraltar Brigade.'"[115]

Perhaps it is Sawyer's official report, written just one day after the battle, that sums up the experience of the Eighth Ohio at Antietam: "During the entire engagement, my officers and men behaved with the utmost bravery and gallantry; not a man gave way....All my officers and men who were present deserve especial mention."[116]

4

"Such an Indefinite Order"

Orders, Confusion and Crook's Ohio Brigade

George Crook's Eleventh, Twenty-Eighth and Thirty-Sixth Ohio Infantry Regiments oozed confidence in themselves and their division when they awoke amid the debris of battle at Fox's Gap on September 15. Lieutenant Colonel Augustus Coleman wrote home, "There is no better division in the field than General Cox's." Crook's men spent much of the day—until 4:00 p.m. by one soldier's watch—examining their field of victory. Reverend William Lyle took a close look at the scores of dead Confederates in the Old Sharpsburg Road. There, they "lay two and three deep, just as they fell!" In the corner of the Wise field, "fifteen Rebel dead lay within a space of three steps!" The Ohioans had ample time to examine their effectiveness of the previous day.[117]

The Ninth Corps left Fox's Gap that afternoon and headed west down the mountain as part of the Army of the Potomac's pursuit of the enemy west, toward the Potomac River. By sunset, they reached the Antietam Valley. The brigade's movements the next day were less defined. Private John D. Kenney of the Eleventh Ohio simply wrote, "The whole day was spent in forming a line of battle." Around nightfall, Crook's men fell into the right center of the corps's line. They spent the night laying in a line of battle, "prepared to move at a moment's notice."[118]

Confidence in Crook's brigade not only ran high through the brigade's own ranks but also in the corps's high command, including Brigadier General Jacob Cox and Major General Ambrose Burnside. Colonel Eliakim Scammon assumed command of the Kanawha Division following

Cox's ascension to corps command because of Reno's death. As the corps assumed its prebattle positions, Burnside determined that if he had to order an attack the next day, the honor of leading belonged to Crook's brigade and the Kanawha Division for their efforts two days prior. McClellan gave the corps the unenviable task of securing a bridge, now known best as the Burnside Bridge, across Antietam Creek, southeast of the town of Sharpsburg. Captain Solomon Teverbaugh, who led some of the first federal troops to probe the enemy defenses at the bridge the next day, called the corps's objective "the hardest task of all."[119]

Colonel George Crook. *Courtesy of the Library of Congress.*

Early on the morning of September 17, Lieutenant Colonel Coleman received orders to monitor the enemy defending the Lower (Burnside) Bridge. Coleman sent Companies C and F forward, to the bluff overlooking the bridge from the east. Captain Teverbaugh, the commander of Company F, recalled that his orders from Coleman were "to watch the enemy very closely; and to immediately inform him or Col. Crook of any movements made by them." After driving a thin Confederate skirmish line across the bridge, Teverbaugh and his men took a glance at the enemy position. On the west bank of the stream, they held "a steep bluff," which the enemy fortified with makeshift breastworks. Their rifles and cannon covered the approaches to the bridge. "The work to be done," one of the Eleventh Ohio men concluded, "was of no ordinary character."[120]

The two companies of the Eleventh Ohio had a few hours to study the terrain leading to the bridge and report their findings to Crook. Between 9:00 and 10:00 a.m., Burnside received orders from army headquarters to begin the assault. He ordered the Eleventh Connecticut to advance toward the bridge and provide covering fire for Crook's men, who were to make the main assault and carry the bridge. A third force under Brigadier General Isaac Rodman headed downstream to cross at a ford below the bridge.[121]

Cox took the responsibility of relaying his plan and orders to Crook. He trusted one of his staff officers, First Lieutenant Samuel Christie, to relay the information. Whether Christie misunderstood the orders and relayed them as such to Crook or if Crook misinterpreted the correct orders is unclear. Nonetheless, when Christie reined his horse alongside Crook, he informed the brigade commander of Cox's order to carry the bridge. As Burnside and Cox reported, their plan was for Crook's attack to be supported by Brigadier General Samuel Sturgis's division. Either Christie or Crook misinterpreted the orders (there is evidence that Christie was not in the best of health during the campaign) and thought Crook was to cross Antietam Creek after Sturgis's division seized the bridge. Despite two companies of the Eleventh Ohio overlooking the bridge for the past two to three hours, Crook asked Christie where the bridge was. According to Crook, Christie responded, "Damned if I know," but he pointed in the direction where he believed it was. Christie provided a similar response to Crook's inquiry about where the creek was. Crook grumbled about "such an indefinite order," to which Christie curtly said, "that he had done his duty in giving the order and it was my [Crook's] duty to obey it." Christie then rode off, "not caring a cent."[122]

The fault for the failure of Crook's brigade to carry out its orders to take the bridge lay at the feet of many. As mentioned above, Crook had two of his companies positioned opposite the bridge's eastern entrance. Their job was to report enemy movements to Crook. Perhaps they simply did that but did not report the bridge's location and surrounding terrain to the brigade commander. Nonetheless, Crook was somehow not aware of where the bridge or creek sat in relation to his brigade's position. Then Crook reiterated three times that he received orders to cross the creek after Sturgis's men had done so. He even said this in his contemporary report, which was written three days after the battle; this directly contrasts Burnside's and Cox's reports. Clearly, their orders to Crook were misconstrued in translation, but whether it was Crook or Christie who misunderstood them remains unclear. According to Crook, Christie misunderstood it.

Once Crook determined to move forward, he took the Eleventh and Twenty-Eighth Ohio Regiments with him and left the Thirty-Sixth Ohio in the rear. Crook sent four companies of the Twenty-Eighth Ohio forward to the hill overlooking the bridge. They did not advance far, however, before Confederate small arms and artillery fire stymied their forward movement. During the advance, Crook saw Union dead in front of the bridge (perhaps from the Eleventh Connecticut). The evidence of a hard fight to carry the bridge and seeing the bridge for the first time himself convinced Crook that it "could not be taken from that point." As far as Crook knew, Sturgis's division had not yet attacked, as he wrongly believed it was supposed to. Thus, he settled into reconnaissance mode. Crook ordered five companies of the Twenty-Eighth Ohio "above the bridge to reconnoiter the enemy's position"

Lieutenant Colonel Augustus Coleman. *Courtesy of the MOLLUS Collection, United States Army Heritage and Education Center, Carlisle, Pennsylvania.*

and sent the rest of the Eleventh Ohio "as skirmishers in the direction of the bridge."[123]

Both advances bogged down in the face of enemy fire. Crook moved half of the Twenty-Eighth Ohio above the bridge as he intended, but it was, perhaps, too far north of the rest of his brigade. They ended up 350 yards north of the bridge and huddled behind a "low sandy ridge and fence" for cover while they fired at Confederate skirmishers across the creek. Lieutenant Colonel Coleman's Eleventh Ohio advanced under the supposition that it was to support its two skirmish companies that were already posted overlooking the bridge. Unfortunately, as the regiment advanced, its left and right wings became separated. The right wing occupied the hill overlooking the bridge and moved no farther from this relatively safe position. Coleman moved the regiment's left wing down to the floodplain of the creek and came within about 100 yards of it. A wall of enemy fire equally stopped this Union formation. Coleman himself fell, mortally wounded, as a bullet shattered his right arm. He died within the hour. Command fell to Major Lyman Jackson. He recognized the regiment's plight and joined its two wings on the hill east of the bridge.[124]

At this moment, Crook ordered a section—two guns—of Simmonds's battery, the Kentucky Light Artillery, into position northeast of the bridge. The other half of the Twenty-Eighth Ohio worked to place and support these guns. However, it took two hours to deploy the pieces. In the meantime, Crook sent word to Cox that "his hands were full, and he could not approach closer to the bridge." The Eleventh and Twenty-Eighth Ohio Regiments fired until their ammunition dried up and the former regiment retired to an orchard in the rear.[125]

Burnside and Cox launched two more attacks to accomplish what they believed Crook should have done. The next attack failed. Shortly after noon, the third attack surged forward. Two regiments, one from New York and one from Pennsylvania in Sturgis's division, attacked the bridge's defenders head on. By this point, the fight for the bridge had raged for over two hours, and the Confederate defenders vainly reached into their nearly empty cartridge boxes for more ammunition. Rodman's force found a place to

Eleventh Ohio monument. *Courtesy of the Library of Congress.*

Left: The monument for McMullin's Ohio battery sits off National Park Service land, along Burnside Bridge Road. *From* The Report of the Ohio Antietam Battlefield Commission.

Opposite, left: Twenty-Eighth Ohio monument. *Courtesy of the Library of Congress.*

Opposite, right: Thirty-Sixth Ohio monument. *Courtesy of the Library of Congress.*

cross downstream of the enemy defenses, and Crook's five Twenty-Eighth Ohio companies found a ford "not over knee deep, with good crossing," upstream of the bridge. Additionally, twelve federal guns fired on the bridge's defenders at close range. This number included two from the Kentucky battery attached to Crook's brigade. After two hours of labor to place the section, one of the howitzers "had a point-blank fire on the farther end of the bridge," according to Cox, and pelted the enemy's position with "double charges of canister." All of these factors conspired against the Confederates, and they abandoned their perch above the bridge at 1:00 p.m.[126]

Crook's brigade joined the corps's surge across the creek. The half of the Twenty-Eighth Ohio that was personally with Crook crossed at the upstream ford, while the rest of the brigade kept their feet dry and marched across the bridge. Except for one company of the Thirty-Sixth Ohio that cleared enemy skirmishers from the Sherrick farm on the creek's west bank, the rest of the brigade reunited and formed line of battle while waiting for their next orders.[127]

For approximately two hours, the Ninth Corps deployed into a mile-long formation two lines deep. It faced west, poised to seize the high ground south and east of Sharpsburg. Crook's men held the right end of the rear line in support of Brigadier General Orlando Willcox's division. Once the corps advanced, Crook's brigade kept close behind the friendly troops in their front. Those troops pressed the Confederates back to the edge of Sharpsburg. The Ohioans charged across a ravine to a stonewall southwest of the Otto farmhouse, while the Eleventh Ohio paused at the Otto farm lane. Crook's two other regiments, the Twenty-Eighth on the left and the Thirty-Sixth on the right, continued toward the wall under heavy enemy shelling.[128]

In a ravine between the lane and the wall, Lieutenant Colonel Melvin Clarke told his Thirty-Sixth Ohio, "Men, lie down, every one of you," as he waved his sword to the ground, indicating his order to those who could not hear him. As his men dropped, Clarke remained upright. Suddenly, a shell from the regiment's left front hit Clarke directly in the "right thigh, at its junction with the hip." Second Lieutenant Wallace Stanley stood near Clarke when the fatal shot hit him. "A shell completely cut one leg off and horribly wounded the other," Stanley wrote six days after the battle. Clarke crumpled to the ground and muttered, "Boys, I'm killed," before he died. "I took his sword and sent it from the field and also his pocketbook and

Top: Major Ebenezer Andrews assumed command of the Thirty-Sixth Ohio in the wake of Clarke's death. *Courtesy of Marietta College Library.*

Bottom: Lieutenant Colonel Melvin Clarke. *Courtesy of L.M. Strayer Collection.*

other things of value," said Stanley. "I found in his vest pocket nearest his heart [a] miniature of a fair-haired little girl, no doubt of his daughter. Little though could that smiling picture see and realize what would have made its original almost shed tears of blood." Crook was behind the Thirty-Sixth Ohio when Clarke fell. He "cast a sad look at his late friend and companion in arms, then took personal charge of the regiment."[129]

Once the two regiments charged uphill to the cover of the stone wall, they did not remain there long. Events elsewhere on the field soon forced Crook's two advanced units to pull back from the zenith of their attack. The Confederate defenders south of Sharpsburg bent—but ultimately did not break—in the face of the Ninth Corps. Portions counterattacked, and Major General A.P. Hill's newly arrived division forced the attack's left flank back, unraveling the whole line. Crook's brigade withdrew to the ridge west of the Burnside Bridge with the rest of the corps, where it occupied the front line in the corps's center.[130]

Crook's brigade went into the Battle of Antietam 2,005 men strong. In the fields on both sides of the creek, the three regiments and Simmonds's Kentucky battery lost 8 men (including two regimental officers); 58 were wounded, and 7 were missing or captured—73 total or 3.6 percent.[131]

The next day did not provide these Ohioans with rest. Skirmishing continued between the opposing lines. Second Lieutenant Alphonso Tiffany's nerves were on edge that morning. "We are all in great suspense," he recorded, "fearing an attack and not force enough to resist much of an attack." Major General George Morell's Fifth Corps division arrived to relieve the corps, which crossed back to the west bank of the stream. Tiffany hoped that the marching and fighting would come to an end. He said he and his comrades needed rest. "We have been marching day and night and exposed to a murderous fire of canister and

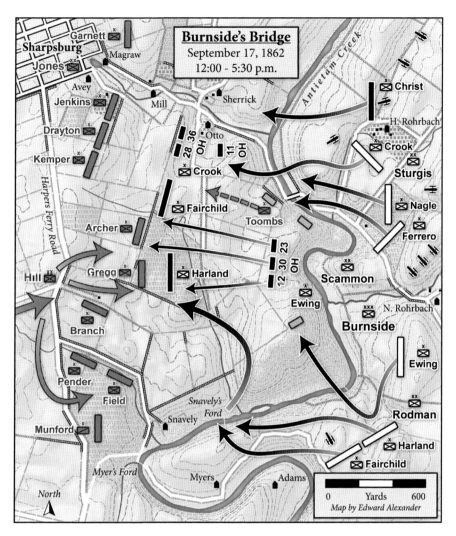

Burnside's Bridge
September 17, 1862
12:00 - 5:30 p.m.

Map by Edward Alexander

The fight for the Burnside Bridge and the final federal attack of the Battle of Antietam. *Courtesy of Edward Alexander.*

shell a great part of the time," Tiffany wrote. "We now feel for the first time in several days that we can rest if we are only permitted to stay here." Thankfully, for Tiffany and his comrades in Crook's brigade, the Maryland Campaign was over.[132]

"WE HAVE DRIVEN THE ENEMY WHEREVER WE HAVE MET THEM"

Ewing's Brigade at Antietam

The soldiers of the Twelfth, Twenty-Third and Thirtieth Ohio Infantry Regiments awoke on the morning of September 15 among the dead and wounded of the Fox's Gap battlefield. "The next morning, I took a stroll to look at the dead Rebels," wrote one member of the Twenty-Third Ohio. "[T]here, in a space of about 8 feet square, laid 15 Rebels, piled up one upon another—in the course of the day, we piled in one heap of dead, found in a lane we charged through, 220 feet long and 20 feet wide, 515 dead Rebels." Samuel Compton remembered a gruesome story years after the battle:

> *As we passed the corner of the little field, astride of the wall was a husky Reb, stone dead, bolt upright, his haversack had fallen in front, both arms extended, palms up and mouth open. Under any circumstances, men will joke. Some "smart Alec" of a Yank had placed a yeast biscuit from his Haversack, one in his mouth and one in each hand. The following was hurled at him. "Say, Johnnie, your [sic] a hog! You need ice, not rations, where you are going! Was that gal good lookin' that baked them are [sic] biscuits. Many more equally rantankerous jibes were hurled at Johnnie.*

The unenviable task of burying the dead consumed much of the morning.[133]

These three regiments endured several hours of sharp fighting the previous day and suffered for it, losing 63 men; 201 were wounded, and 8 were missing.

Colonel Hugh Ewing. *Courtesy of the Library of Congress.*

Additionally, the loss of corps commander Major General Jesse Reno bumped officers up the command chain; Colonel Hugh Ewing then led the brigade, and Lieutenant Colonel Theodore Jones assumed command of the Thirtieth Ohio in Ewing's stead.[134]

Hugh Boyle Ewing was part of Ohio's prominent Ewing family and, thus, was William Tecumseh Sherman's foster brother. Born on October 31, 1826, Ewing entered the United States Military Academy at West Point in 1844. He did not, however, graduate from the academy. Bullies, including Ewing's future superior officer Ambrose Burnside, tainted Ewing's experience, and he became depressed. He ignored his studies and failed out of the school in his senior year. Ewing participated in the westward surge toward California during the gold rush before he settled down in Missouri and Kansas as a lawyer. Ohio called him home prior to the outbreak of hostilities in 1861, and Ewing quickly offered his services at the beginning of the war. Before reaching Maryland, he served in western Virginia.[135]

After receiving rations and burying as many of the dead at Fox's Gap as they could, Ewing's brigade, along with the rest of the Ninth Corps, marched west from South Mountain in the evening and reached the east bank of Antietam Creek by sundown. Once the rising sun illuminated the landscape, Ewing's men came under Confederate artillery fire. While making coffee, Edward Schweitzer and his comrades heard "a cannon ball come whizzing." They tracked the quick trajectory of the shot and vainly attempted to avoid it. Two men fell victim to the errant shot; it wounded Private William Bowers and ripped the leg off of Corporal David Taylor. Despite the losses and continued shelling, Schweitzer and the men of the Thirtieth Ohio enjoyed watching this deadly ball be retrieved by the nearby artillerymen of Lieutenant Samuel Benjamin's Battery E, Second United States Artillery, who fired it back at the enemy. The brigade did not move until the evening, when it assumed a position east of Antietam Creek's lower bridge, again in support of Lieutenant Benjamin's guns.[136]

The dawn of September 17 brought more enemy artillery shells raining down on the men under Ewing's command. Though it made them uncomfortable, Major George Hildt proudly reported that the men lay under cover and suffered no casualties. The fight for the possession of the Lower (Burnside) Bridge began between 9:00 and 10:00 a.m. While the federals directly stormed the bridge for the next three hours, Ewing's brigade joined Brigadier General Isaac Rodman's division in a movement to get around the Confederate defenders by crossing Antietam Creek at a ford below the bridge. "About 10 o'clock, we started to the left and front," wrote Lieutenant Henry Brinkerhoff of the Thirtieth Ohio. This flanking column was supposed to be near the ford it intended to cross, but that ford was impracticable to use for a column of 3,200 infantry. Rodman's and Ewing's men thus continued marching downstream to find a suitable crossing point. After marching "two miles over very rough ground"—"a zigzag march, behind hills and along ravines," said Lieutenant Brinkerhoff—the column began crossing the creek at about 1:00 p.m., Rodman's division at Snavely's Ford and Ewing's brigade at a bend in the Antietam Creek, upstream from the ford. The crossing went off rather smoothly, despite Confederate artillery harassing it. "The water came to my armpits," said the Twelfth Ohio's Samuel Compton, "and I had to hold my haversack and cartridge box up over my head." Ewing's brigade moved north and west from the ford before deploying on the left of the forming federal line.[137]

Ewing's men continued to suffer from the Confederate artillery on their march into position. However, along the way, they also found suffering

A postwar view of Snavely's Ford. *From* The Report of the Ohio Antietam Battlefield Commission.

enemy artillerists. They had gathered around a pile of straw that had caught fire from the shell of a Union battery, and it "burned [them] to death," remembered Colonel Ewing. The Ohioans threw their blankets "over the charred remains" to hide the grisly scene. They found more wounded Confederates under a tree, which the Ohio surgeons quickly attended. Suddenly, the enemy artillery fire resumed and killed sixteen of the enemy's wounded, including one "whose leg, at the moment, was being amputated."[138]

Elsewhere along the line of Ewing's brigade, the enemy artillery continued to annoy the Buckeye soldiers. After the battle, one Twenty-Third Ohio soldier revealed the type of ammunition the Confederates fired during this phase of the battle. "The Rebels are entirely out of ammunition," he wrote home. "At Sharpsburgh, one of the Thirtieth Ohio was shot through the leg with a sledgehammer thrown from the Rebel artillery. Horseshoes, doorknobs, buttons and such like articles were taken out of our wounded, which goes to show their want of ammunition." The division commander, Colonel Eliakim Scammon, reined up his horse in front of the Twenty-Third Ohio during the shelling and demanded to know, "Why is my brigade being exposed in this way?" He barked out orders; "we rushed behind a hill," noted Private Edward Henry, "and hundreds of lives were saved from the terrible fire." There, the brigade waited for its order to advance in the final federal assault of September 17.[139]

Corps commander Brigadier General Jacob Cox gave the order to advance at 3:15 p.m. Soon, approximately eight thousand blue-clad soldiers marched forward to strike the enemy just south of Sharpsburg. Ewing's brigade did not have far to march, as it assumed a reserve position during the attack. But about one hour into the assault, Confederate troops broke the left of the Union front line in a forty-acre cornfield. Ewing's Ohioans moved forward to blunt the enemy onslaught. Major James Comly's Twenty-Third Ohio held the brigade's right, Lieutenant Colonel Theodore Jones's Thirtieth Ohio occupied the center, and the Twelfth Ohio, under the command of Colonel Carr White, was on the left of the line.

Ewing's advance unraveled quickly. Before the brigade advanced, reports of an enemy force moving around its left prompted Ewing to order White's two-hundred-man Twelfth Ohio to face south, perpendicular to the line of the Twenty-Third and Thirtieth Regiments. White's regiment moved into the cornfield but immediately came under enemy artillery and infantry fire. Worse yet, the Twelfth Ohio was caught in the crossfire of opposing enemy and friendly batteries and suffered damage from both. A green Union regiment, no doubt panicked, likewise opened fire into White's line.

Twelfth Ohio monument. *Courtesy of the Library of Congress.*

White ordered his men to hit the ground to escape their deadly predicament. He asked for a volunteer to run the gauntlet of fire to tell the friendly units to their rear to cease fire. Company F's Sergeant John M. Snook volunteered to go. In the meantime, White yelled for his regiment to move to the left, an order that was misunderstood by part of the line and nearly resulted in the regiment breaking for the rear. It did not break, however, and ultimately assumed a position in the Otto farm lane on the east edge of the cornfield, where it exchanged a long-range fire with the enemy. The regiment lost six men, and twenty-four were wounded, mostly from hostile artillery fire.[140]

Without the Twelfth Ohio, Ewing's other two regiments advanced westward to shore up the federal left flank. As soon as both regiments crested the ridge east of the Otto farm lane, they came under fire. At double-quick, both regiments plunged forward, toward a stone wall on the west end of the cornfield. Comly's Twenty-Third Ohio had the advantage of moving over open ground north of the cornfield. Jones's Thirtieth Ohio was not as fortunate. They moved partially across a plowed field and through the corn. By the time they reached the wall, "our men, at this time, were utterly exhausted," reported Major Hildt. Huddling behind the wall, the men's "fire was necessarily slow and desultory for several minutes."[141]

Thirtieth Ohio monument. *Courtesy of the Library of Congress.*

Left: Major James Comly. *Courtesy of the Rutherford B. Hayes Presidential Library and Museum.*

Right: Twenty-Third Ohio monument. *Courtesy of the Library of Congress.*

Alexander Wight, a musician in the Twenty-Third Ohio who was performing as a stretcher bearer at Antietam, noted how the stone wall protected the Ohioans. It "served well as a fort and but few were killed, although a great many were wounded in their arms and hands, some in the shoulder and different places," he said. As soon as both regiments reached the fence, they opened fire into the men of Archer's and Toombs's Confederate brigades in their front. During their advance, Archer's brigade lost one-third of its men, a testament to the deadly work being performed by Ewing's two regiments.[142]

While the Ohioans quickly checked the enemy in their front, it was their left flank that suddenly became the crisis point. After firing a volley into Archer's and Toombs's men, "a withering fire" struck the left of the Thirtieth Ohio. This fire came from elements of Brigadier General Maxcy Gregg's brigade. The Twenty-Third Ohio did not initially offer support, believing the enemy to be friendly troops. "The Rebels were seen coming down upon us, but were mistaken for our men, they having our flag flying and was dressed in our uniform," reported one member of the regiment. But once this flanking fire plunged into Comly's regiment as well, the identity of the troops who fired could not be mistaken. "We were brought under a heavy crossfire," one of Comly's men wrote home, "which is a very unpleasant position to be in." Indeed, it was, and Ewing and Comly recognized that fact quickly.[143]

Colonel Ewing immediately ordered the two regiments to face this new threat. The Twenty-Third Ohio and the four right companies of the Thirtieth Ohio followed Ewing's directive; the remainder of the Thirtieth Ohio did not hear the order above the din of battle. Ewing sent Lieutenant Reese Furbay of his staff into the fray to order the rest of the Thirtieth Ohio back, but Furbay fell dead in the attempt. The enemy's flank fire continued to harass the remaining companies. After suffering more losses, including two color-bearers, the six left companies of the Thirtieth Ohio fell back from the stone fence.

They did so just as Archer's men reached the other side. A few plucky Confederates temporarily charged across the fence and captured Lieutenant Colonel Theodore Jones. Soon, more of Archer's soldiers charged into the cornfield, but the Thirtieth Ohio's six wayward companies stopped them cold. By this point, the rest of the Twenty-Third and Thirtieth Ohio had quit the field. By facing south, they exposed their right flank to Archer's and Toombs's brigade that was advancing from the west. The fight for Ewing's brigade was over on September 17.[144]

Lieutenant Colonel Theodore Jones. *Courtesy of the MOLLUS Collection, United States Army Heritage and Education Center, Carlisle, Pennsylvania.*

The brigade fought for about one hour on that bloody Wednesday. It carried 1,180 men into action and lost 28 officers and men; 134 were wounded, and 18 were captured or missing for a total of 182 (15.4 percent) casualties. A majority of the casualties came from the Twenty-Third and Thirtieth Ohio Regiments, which were flanked twice during the action and surprisingly did not suffer heavier losses. Still, the enemy subjected these two regiments to intense musketry during the action in and around the forty-acre cornfield.[145]

After engaging in two major battles within a span of four days, Ewing's brigade took stock of what it had lost. Private Albert Logan of Comapny E, Twenty-Third Ohio, wrote that a second lieutenant then led his company and that his company's captain

Colors of the Twenty-Third Ohio. *Courtesy of the MOLLUS Collection, United States Army Heritage and Education Center, Carlisle, Pennsylvania.*

was second in charge of the regiment. But the Rebel bullets did not only hit Ohio officers. "Our flag is a curiosity," said one Twenty-Third Ohio soldier about his regiment's flag after the two battles. "[T]he whole of the blue field, except the last row of stars, is shot away, and the flag is completely in ribbons." With so many bullets piercing the flag, the regiment's flag bearer, Sergeant Joshua Armstrong, was killed from a ball, "which had struck the standard" before it "pierced the standard-bearer to the heart, and he fell, wrapped in the folds of the banner he had loved and borne so well; it was literally dyed with his blood." At South Mountain three days prior, Armstrong had been reported killed. "I tell you, no one can carry [the flag] and live," said one of Armstrong's comrades after learning that the rumors were false. "Then I'll carry it and die," Armstrong replied. His prophecy came true. He was buried in Antietam National Cemetery, grave number 1,326.[146]

Three days after the action at Antietam, as the Maryland Campaign ended, Hugh Ewing finally had a chance to write to his wife. "I have passed unhurt, thank God, through almost uninterrupted danger," he began. "I have lost very many of my best men and officers—on the 17th, two of my aids were killed, and the third had his horse shot under him." Despite the shock and horror of fighting two major battles in less than one week, Ewing proclaimed, "We have driven the enemy wherever we have met them, but our loss is heavy and we are worn almost to death." If anyone in the Army of the Potomac deserved a respite following the Maryland Campaign, it was the men of Ewing's brigade.[147]

"A Sight Terrible Beyond All Conception"

Ohioans and the Aftermath of Battle

While the sun worked through its daily positions across the sky on September 17, the Battle of Antietam raged. Early streaks of light that morning found combatants already engaged on the Confederate left flank on the northern end of the battlefield. The battle continued to shift southward during the day. From midmorning through early afternoon, intense fighting centered on the middle of the Confederate army's battle line. Well into the afternoon, the federal army finally got a long-delayed attack moving forward, toward the Confederate army's right flank. With the battlefront so far south from where combat had begun so many hours earlier, many soldiers on both sides took stock of the enormity of the fight and the scars it left on the landscape and both armies. The desperate and intense fighting of the morning and early afternoon only produced the beginning of a tragic aftermath to the day's engagement while the battle still raged. Those Buckeyes who fought during the early hours of the battle were some of the first Ohioans to see the true cost of the battle.

Captain Frederick A. Seymour of the Seventh Ohio had already seen heavy combat earlier in the day around the Dunker Church and in the West Woods. While the sound of gunfire was still audible from the south, Seymour took in the awful scenes around their position and some of the no-man's-land between the two lines. "The dead lying mangled and torn in all the horrid ghastliness of death was a sight terrible beyond all conception," he wrote. Noting the wounded around him, he observed "Rebel and Union soldiers lay side by side, apparently forgetting they ever were enemies, piteously asking for water and help from those who, a short half hour ago, were seeking each other's life with all the intensity of hatred which man is capable." Seymour came across a wounded Confederate officer and immediately offered him some water. The officer's eyes dampened as he responded in the affirmative, having felt convinced just moments earlier that Seymour was approaching to bayonet the wounded man. Private Robert S. Bower, also of the Seventh Ohio, agreed with Seymour on the horrible aftermath of the fighting. While walking in the area of Miller's now-infamous cornfield, taking in the sights of heavy fighting earlier that day, Bower recalled in a letter dated September 18, "I never saw as many killed and wounded in my life as there were of the Rebels where we first met them. It was almost impossible to walk over the ground without stepping on them."[148]

To the left of the Seventh Ohio's position, Surgeon Thomas M. Ebright vividly recalled the first Confederate casualties brought to his care. Not only were these the more grievously wounded Confederate soldiers from the Eighth Ohio's area of operations, but, according to Ebright, they represented the true condition of General Robert E. Lee's Army of Northern Virginia. Written one week after the battle, Ebright recalled in a letter, "The Rebels, especially, were objects of my especial commiseration. The extreme wounded were those generally obtained by us, and their dirty, haggard appearance, aside from their mangled limbs and contused bodies, is not the most pleasant to look upon."[149]

The battle finally came to an end. Each side stared, waited and looked for signs of a resumption of the fight. It never came. Darkness settled across the landscape, creating an even more macabre scene that became seared into the minds of many veterans for the rest of their lives. While the cacophony of battle decreased into sporadic musket fire in the growing darkness, temporary aid stations and improvised field hospitals were overflowing with patients, as more wounded were being retrieved from the field. Musician Alexander Wight of the Twenty-Third Ohio wrote a letter to his brother on September 26. In it, he revealed his support for Major General George B. McClellan's handling of the army during the campaign and the most recent battle. McClellan's reputation for taking care of the men under his command was also on display on the evening of September 17. "You may think I am crazy, but I have seen something since I came here that convinces me that McClellan is doing all he can for his and our country," Wight wrote. Earlier that day, Wight told his brother that he "was helping a wounded man off the field, and he [McClellan] rode up to me and asked me if he was badly wounded and if he could ride. He jumped off his horse and helped me to put the man on, but he could not ride." Further strengthening Wight's support of McClellan was another incident he witnessed that evening as the work was increasing for the surgeons and medical staff in the field hospitals that were popping up across the battlefield landscape. "That night after the fight, they [McClellan and Burnside] visited the hospitals and spoke to the boys like a father and told them that they had done well and gained a great victory," Wight shared. "He did not just go in and speak, but he went to the boys and shook hands with them and spoke to them like a father."

Wight recalled the horrors he saw on the field. Of the Confederates killed outright, he said they "were lying by platoons and divisions. I could scarcely get through the field without tramping on them....they were lying thick all over." Wight also confided in his brother the destruction that artillery fire could do to the human body and how he dealt with seeing it firsthand that afternoon. He saw "men torn to pieces with cannon balls or shell, burned to death by the explosion of magazines, some with their head and shoulders torn off, some their legs some cut in two in the middle, and every other way, it is a terrible sight. I could not stand it had I not got some used to seeing dead and wounded men before in the afternoon."[150]

While many like Wight worked throughout the evening to bring in the wounded and attempt to save as many as possible, there were others who were thankful that the fighting was done—at least for the night. A vast majority of the Army of the Potomac slept on the battlefield that night, including the Buckeyes in the Twelfth Ohio Infantry. After two battles in four days, these men, including Private Samuel Compton, were exhausted. As the darkness of night deepened and the temperatures slowly dropped, the men of the Twelfth "slept in ranks on the battlefield." Being "a cool September night," wrote Compton, sleeping on the ground was "not conducive to sleep." The cold was simply too much for this Ohioan. With his teeth chattering and his limbs shaking from chills, he went "out on the battlefield [to] see if I could find a blanket. The moon was looking on the bloody field with complacency as if kids had been playing hide and seek." Soon, however, Compton's search for warmth led him to discover the battle's terrible aftermath. "I had not gone a half [dozen] rods when I saw a mound covered with blanket, [and] going up and removing the blanket, I found the mound was made up of two corpes [sic], one shattered by a shell 'till it had but little resemblance to humanity. The other cut in two by a cannonball looked still more ghastly. Of course, I left that blanket alone." He pressed on in his search, "Seeing another not far away, I started towards it. Now I have it, I thought, putting my hand down to grasp, I found it as though it had been soaked all day in blood." It would be a long, cold and traumatic evening for Samuel Compton.[151]

By the morning of September 18, 1862, many more wounded men had been retrieved from the battlefield and taken to the numerous aid stations and field hospitals that dotted the rear of the main battle lines. Wounded Ohioans from the various units on the field who had participated in the battle then faced their next fight—their fight to live. The experiences of these Buckeyes widely varied. Although Dr. Jonathan Letterman, the medical director of the Army of the Potomac, worked feverishly to rebuild, reequip and improve the efficiency of his medical department and its staff after the Peninsula Campaign earlier that summer, his new system, later known as the Letterman System, did not operate perfectly following this battle.

Wounded in the fight for the Bloody Lane, Azor Nickerson of the Eighth Ohio made it back to where his unit had initially gone into position earlier on September 17. There, a field hospital had been organized among the several farm buildings that were owned by the Roulette family. Nickerson described what met his eyes on September 17 over thirty years after the battle. When he reached the hospital for treatment on his gunshot wound to the shoulder, "the sight was appalling. It seemed as though nearly the whole of my regiment was there." Not only did the number of wounded men from his regiment affect him, but the grievous nature of their wounds further haunted his memory. "Three of my lieutenant comrades with their eyes shot out and poor Lieutenant [Charles W.] Barnes with an awful wound in the head, from which a portion of his brain protruded," remembered Nickerson. Sadly, the next day, when the ambulances arrived and Barnes got up to walk to one of them, he collapsed after a few steps, dead.[152]

One of the surgeons at the Roulette Field Hospital was Surgeon Ebright. He agreed with Nickerson about the scene that was then taking place at the field hospital, writing that the "scenes of horror and suffering…would appall the most hardened in the shedding of blood." Working out of the Roulette barn itself, "where I had my operative depot," Ebright relayed the "scene of misery" he witnessed for the first week after the battle. "[Here] were mingled the lacerated and maimed from all parts of the world, mingling their plaintive cries and dying groans….The cry was Dr. here and everywhere help implored. The wailing sound dies but slowly in my ears, and my dreams are oft disturbed by revisions of the sights which make even victory sad," he concluded.[153]

Nickerson did not stay at the Roulette farm for long. He then went to the Keedysville Church Hospital for further treatment. The sight there was even

The Roulette Farm. *Courtesy of the Library of Congress.*

more disturbing. "The wounded were lying in the little grove that partially surrounded the church, each poor wretch waiting his turn for examination," he wrote. It was finally his turn to see the hospital surgeon.

> *When my turn came, they took me up to a seat that stood facing the pulpit but perpendicular to the others and near which was an open window. As we walked up the aisle, we splashed along in the blood that had run down from the amputations that lay on boards placed on the pews on either side. The operating surgeons were in their shirtsleeves, which were rolled up, leaving their bare arms exposed and covered with blood, giving them the appearance of a bevy of butchers in a Chicago abattoir. While sitting awaiting the surgeon, every few minutes, an attendant would bring past me, to the open window, an arm, a leg, or a mangled hand, which he pitched into a little trench dug under the window for the purpose.*[154]

There were other Ohioans who were on the move on September 18 who witnessed the many impromptu field hospitals and the treatment of the wounded inside them. First Lieutenant Harlow N. Spencer of the Seventh Ohio was just one who recorded what he saw of the hospitals that September day. Having only been in federal military service just shy of four weeks at the time of the battle, Spencer, in a letter to a friend on September 29, recalled passing through "the village of Boonsboro, the churches and many other buildings were opened as hospitals, and the ladies were rapidly passing to and fro, ministering to the wounded." As other Buckeye units were on the move in the days after the battle they, like Spencer, witnessed numerous other scars to the local towns and villages beyond their public and private buildings being pressed into hospital service. Just a day later, on September 19, Frederick Seymour recorded in a letter that the town of Sharpsburg "looked as if some terrible earthquake had visited it, so torn and shattered was it with shot and shell." When Surgeon Ebright was finally able to get to the town after nonstop work at the Roulette farm, he noticed that Sharpsburg "was sadly cut up, all most [*sic*] every house in it gives evidence of the destructive character of the missiles that were rained upon it, shattering its walls, demolishing its chimneys and compelling the inhabitants to seek shelter in the cellars." According to those in Sharpsburg, Ebright later shared in his letter, "fortunately, none of the citizens were hurt, save one little girl killed by a piece of shell." Perhaps it was a letter from a soldier in the Twenty-Third Ohio written a week after the battle that best encapsulated the impact the aftermath had on the surrounding countryside. Published in the *Cleveland Plain Dealer*, the letter reported, "The inhabitants of this part of the country are suffering for want of food. During the stay of the Rebel army here, they subsisted on the loyal citizens, and what was not given to them, they took."[155]

The battle had completely transformed the landscape around Sharpsburg, Maryland. Thousands of wounded from both sides had been taken to field hospitals, aid stations and public and private buildings that had been turned into temporary hospitals. The fighting trampled, bloodied and spoiled dozens of acres of farm fields, standing crops and orchards. Artillery and musket fire damaged houses, barns, outbuildings and structures in the town of Sharpsburg proper. But it was the thousands of dead soldiers strewn about the battlefield that not only created a health crisis for the surrounding area, but left the deepest impact on the men who witnessed the tragic toll of war.

Daylight broke on September 18, 1862, with many in the Army of the Potomac awaiting a renewal in the previous day's battle. The hours ticked by with no renewal. With signs not pointing to further battle, federal regiments sent out details to collect and bury their dead and search for any remaining wounded or missing. Captain Frederick Seymour recalled this duty with his unit. "On arriving at the point where our men had fallen," Seymour related, "we collected all we knew to have been killed, took them to a burying ground neatly enclosed, and there, in their soldier's grave, put up a headboard to their graves, dropped a tear over their ashes, and bid them farewell." Others selected for this grim task also wrote of their experience collecting and burying their dead. On October 22, 1862, an article by "Julius" appeared in the *Western Reserve Chronicle* titled "From the Seventh." This soldier's account of burial detail surely shocked the readers back home who were living in the Western Reserve. Julius described "the dead and wounded lay[ing] in an indiscriminate pile and in numbers difficult to imagine. The blood lay in pools or ran in crimson streams." The task before this soldier left an indelible imprint on his memory.

> *To clear the bodies, I had to stand upon the top of the fence and jump as far as I could. All over the field, the dead lay in long rows, plainly showing the position of every line of battle. Some idea may be gained of the immense slaughter by the fact that on an area of only 700 square feet, with a front of 60,* fifty-seven dead bodies lay besides the proportionate number of wounded. *This was immediately in front of our regiment in the first engagement....The slaughter was terrible in the extreme.*[156]

Over the next several days, Julius had more time to walk over the battlefield, and at every step, he continued to see the dead who were yet to be buried, scenes that were "too horrible" to describe. What he saw during those late September days would never be forgotten. "I shall always remember those upturned, disfigured and blackened faces, everywhere to be seen upon the field, along the road through the village of Sharpsburg, out to the bridge taken by Gen. Burnside, and the thousand other painful scenes," he wrote. Private John Hume, also of the Seventh Ohio, agreed with Julius on the horrors left behind on the battlefield. In a letter to a friend dated September 21, Hume described what he saw of the Rebel dead just a day after the battle. "[T]hey lay as thick as they can lay. Some places, in piles you have no idea how many dead there is unless you seen it. I can't half describe it to you. You would think it could not be, sir," he confided to his friend. "[T]hey lay for a mile all along the battle line that if they were regular, you could not go the length of it without stepping on a dead body."[157]

The Maryland Campaign had yet to come to a conclusion in the immediate days after the battle. The Army of the Potomac, in response to the Army of Northern Virginia's retreat back toward Virginia, was on the move. But not all of the federal soldiers were to go with the Army of the Potomac in its pursuit of General Lee. Thomas Francis Galwey of the Eighth Ohio

Infantry recalled as the army was in pursuit on Saturday, September 20, "Our corps, the Second, is retained to bury the dead....The stench from the dead, both horses and men, is something frightful." The following day, Sunday, their "work of burying dead" continued. The larger work of repairing the shattered landscape, clearing away the detritus of battle and healing the wounds created on September 17, 1862, had just begun.[158]

7

Ohioans at Rest in Antietam National Cemetery

With the battle and the evacuation of the wounded over, burying the dead was the next task for the Union army. The Confederate army was in full retreat, and the grisly task fell solely to the men in the Army of the Potomac. All recognized the danger that bodies lying unburied presented to the health of those in the area. They had to be buried—and buried quickly. It was yet another immense challenge, as 3,600 soldiers had been killed in the battle. Because of the need to bury them quickly and the amount to be buried, soldiers were often buried in long, shallow trenches. For those who saw the dead on the battlefield in the days after the battle or for those soldiers who were detailed to bury them, it was a sight they never forgot.

"In every direction around, men were digging graves and burying the dead," Lieutenant Colonel David Hunter Strother, a Union staff officer, wrote. "Ten or twelve bodies lay at the different pits and had already become offensive....Many were black...heads and faces hideously swelled, covered with dust until they looked like clods." Burying the decomposing remains were soldiers like Lieutenant Origen G. Bingham of the 137th Pennsylvania Infantry. Bingham's unit did not fight in the battle, but following the action, it was ordered to bury the Confederate dead. It was "the most disagreeable duty that could have been assigned to us," he wrote home. "[Tongue] cannot describe the horrible sight which we have witnessed....I would not describe to you the appearance of the dead even if I could; it is too revolting. You can imagine the condition of the bodies when I tell you that they were slain on Wednesday and it is now Sunday."[159]

These graves dotted the landscape around Sharpsburg for four years until October 1866, when work began on the removal of the dead and their reburial in Antietam National Cemetery, a project that had begun two years earlier. In 1864, legislation was passed to create a national cemetery to bury the remains of soldiers who had died in the Battle of Antietam, though it was later decided to only bury Union remains in the cemetery. The next step was to purchase a suitable piece of land for the cemetery. Maryland donated $5,000 toward this effort. The project hit an early roadblock in working with the landowner. To circumvent this roadblock, the Maryland legislature passed legislation repealing the original act, and in March 1865, additional legislation was passed to provide for the purchase of eleven acres of land. This time, Maryland would not work alone, as other state representatives and those from Maryland formed "a body politic in law, under the name, style and title of the Antietam National Cemetery." An additional $7,000 was appropriated for the project as well.[160]

It was the duty of all involved, including the state trustees, to remove the remains of all soldiers from the battlefields of Antietam and South Mountain. It was then decided that the remains of the Confederate casualties would be buried on a portion of the ground separate from the Union casualties. Eventually, eighteen other states, all from the Union, joined the Antietam National Cemetery Corporation. These states included Connecticut, Delaware, Illinois, Indiana, Iowa, Maine, Massachusetts, Michigan, Minnesota, New Hampshire, New Jersey, New York, Ohio, Pennsylvania, Rhode Island, Vermont, West Virginia and Wisconsin. When the cemetery was completed, these states had contributed over $90,000 and changed the purpose and scope of the cemetery.

A local resident of Sharpsburg, Aaron Good, helped make a list of burial places. He had already devoted his time to identifying the dead and locating their graves before work on the cemetery began. The community of Sharpsburg was overwhelmed by the battle, and quick burials in shallow trenches had been the rule. Although some bodies had been embalmed and others buried in natural conditions that preserved the remains, by 1865, only skeletons remained in most of the trenches. Good's work greatly helped in identifying the dead as their remains were reinterred in the newly created cemetery. On September 17, 1867, five years after the battle that had forever changed so many lives and the course of our nation, the cemetery was officially dedicated to those who "gave the last full measure of devotion."[161]

Today, many Ohioans are buried in Antietam National Cemetery. There are those who were killed outright during the fighting at South Mountain and Antietam, buried near where they had fallen and later removed to the cemetery during the second half of the 1860s. Other Ohioans who rest in the national cemetery today succumbed to grievous wounds, failed medical procedures or illness contracted during the campaign. Each one of these men who lie beneath their neatly aligned headstones have an individual story to tell. Taken together, these stories tell the larger experience of Ohioans at South Mountain, Antietam and during the Maryland Campaign.

For those Ohioans in the Army of the Potomac that September, their first engagement of the campaign, which began on September 4, 1862, did not occur until the Battle of South Mountain on September 14. Private Spencer Cherington of the Thirty-Sixth Ohio Infantry fell during the fighting. He enlisted as a private in Company K of the unit just a year prior, in August 1861, at the age of twenty-seven. His death was taken especially hard at home, where he left behind his wife, Susan, of almost five years and two young children. His third and last child, Margaret, was born in January 1863; Susan was almost six months pregnant when she learned that Spencer had been killed in action. Originally buried in nearby Frederick, Maryland, his remains were reinterred in Antietam National Cemetery in 1867.[162]

Two others who were killed in action at South Mountain on September 14, 1862, and later reinterred in the national cemetery were John Baker and George W. Detrick. The tragedy of Baker's death was his age at the time of the battle. He joined the Eleventh Ohio Infantry not even eight months before his death at the age of sixteen. George Detrick was an experienced veteran when he was killed in combat at Fox's Gap. He enlisted in Company F, Twenty-Third Ohio, in the late spring of 1861, when patriotic fervor and war fever swept through the country. After George enlisted in the state's capital, Columbus, at the age of twenty-two, his brother Samuel also joined the federal war effort, later enlisting in the Sixty-Third Pennsylvania. Today, the remains of John Baker and George W. Detrick lie not far from each other in grave numbers 1,420 and 1,409, respectively.[163]

There were many Ohioans who had been wounded during the Battle of South Mountain and lingered for weeks before finally succumbing to their injuries. Although they were evacuated from the battlefield, taken to general hospitals in nearby Maryland towns and received medical treatment and care for their wounds, they were sadly unable to win their battle of recovery. During the fighting on September 14, a new nineteen-year-old recruit, John W. Hoover, received a gunshot wound to his leg. Hoover, who had enlisted in Company K, Thirty-Sixth Ohio Infantry, just two and a half months earlier, was taken to a hospital in nearby Frederick. Two days after being wounded,

Right: Private Spencer Cherrington, Thirty-Sixth Ohio Infantry. Killed in action on September 14, 1862. Grave no. 1498, Antietam National Cemetery. *Courtesy of Jon Tracey.*

Below: George Detrick (*left*) Twenty-Third Ohio Infantry, killed in action at the Battle of South Mountain. *Courtesy of the Library of Congress.*

his leg was amputated due to the wound's severity. It was a wound and operation that he would not recover from. He died on October 6, 1862.[164]

Two other Ohioans who were wounded in the fight at Fox's Gap were brothers William and John Noble. The Noble brothers both enlisted in the Thirtieth Ohio Infantry in the late summer and early fall of 1861. William, the younger of the two, joined Company D in the middle of August 1861 at the age of nineteen, while twenty-nine-year-old John did not enlist in the same company until the early days of September 1861. Both were mortally wounded during the Battle of South Mountain, and both were evacuated to hospitals in Frederick. John's grievous leg wound required the amputation of the limb shortly after arriving at U.S. Army General Hospital No. 5. At some point during his convalescence following the amputation, John's wound developed an infection that he did not recover from. He died on October 15, 1862. Sadly, much like when the younger Noble brother led the way by enlisting before his brother John, William was first in death. Following his mortal wound on September 14, William was taken to a hospital in Middletown, Maryland. The brothers last saw each other at the height of combat at Fox's Gap and in the moments they laid on the field following their wounding. William died four days before John, on October 11. Today, you can find John at gravesite 1,499 and his brother William at gravesite 1,403 at Antietam National Cemetery.[165]

For students of the Battle of Antietam, the battle began with the predawn light in Miller's cornfield. By and large, the historiography of the engagement over much of the twentieth century has well established that narrative. But there was fighting between the opposing lines before that fateful morning of September 17, and for Ohio, it led to the loss of another of its sons.

David Taylor enlisted in Company I, Thirtieth Ohio Infantry, during the war's first summer, on August 22, 1861. Within ten months, Taylor was promoted to the rank of corporal. On September 16, he was killed in action. Lieutenant Henry Brinkerhoff of the Thirtieth Ohio, who wrote the unit's regimental history, recorded the events that led to Taylor's mortal wounding. "On the sixteenth, a regular battery of thirty-two-pounders [*sic*], commanded by Lieut. Benjamin, was planted on an eminence a short distance in front of our line," Brinkerhoff recorded just months later. "This battery, throughout the entire day, was shelling the enemy's position; and occasional replies from the rebel batteries were provoked, and almost invariably, the balls over shot the battery and came down in our camps. Several conical shot fell near our regiment, and finally, one struck directly in the line, knocking a stack of muskets in all directions, and killed Corporal David Taylor and wounded

Left: Private William Noble, Thirtieth Ohio Infantry. Mortally wounded on September 14, 1862, died on October 11, 1862. Grave no. 1403, Antietam National Cemetery. *Courtesy of Jon Tracey.*

Right: Private John Noble, Thirtieth Ohio Infantry. Mortally wounded on September 14, 1862, died on October 15, 1862. Grave no. 1499, Antietam National Cemetery. *Courtesy of Jon Tracey.*

private William S. Bowers of Company I." Today, Taylor rests in grave site 1,366 in Antietam National Cemetery.[166]

A day after Taylor's death, on September 17, the heaviest fighting of the Maryland Campaign occurred. Ohioans were heavily engaged in combat during the Battle of Antietam, later to receive the title as America's single bloodiest day.

Like so many others, Charles Hosmer Wright was swept up with war fever during the war's first summer. Born and raised in Concord, Massachusetts, he later lived in the towns of Lowell and Cambridge before settling in Lawrence, Massachusetts. There, Charles owned and operated a shoe store, but he did not stay long in that profession, nor in Massachusetts. When the Civil War began in earnest in April 1861, Charles was living in Bowling Green, Kentucky, where he worked with the *Bowling Green Gazette.* Charles had noted "that the location was rather hot for a gentleman of strong northern sentiments," and thus, he struck out for Ohio and enlistment. On June 19, 1861, he enlisted at Camp Dennison into Company K, Eleventh

Ohio Infantry, and as his company was being organized, he was appointed as its corporal. During the unit's service in western Virginia, he applied his previous trade and published the *Eleventh Ohio* camp newspaper, much to the delight of his comrades. An older soldier in the ranks, Wright was killed in action on September 17 at the age of thirty-wo. Although his remains were later moved to Sleepy Hollow Cemetery in his hometown of Concord, his service in the Eleventh Ohio, a service to both the Buckeye state and the federal armies, would not be forgotten. His name was later added to a monument in Concord that lists all of the city's native sons who fought in the various units of federal service during the American Civil War.[167]

Much like Charles Wright, John Lantry's remains did not stay on the Antietam battlefield. At the age of twenty-six, on June 18, 1861, John Lantry enlisted in Company B, Eighth Ohio Infantry, as a second lieutenant. During the Eighth Ohio's attack on the Sunken Road—an already naturally strong position—the Eighth Ohio suffered numerous casualties. Of the 324 men the regiment brought into the fight, 165 of them were killed, wounded or captured. Among the dead from the Eighth Ohio was John Lantry. Although he was born in Ireland, John and the rest of his family had made Cleveland, Ohio, their home. Following the news of John's death at the battle, his brother James departed from Cleveland in search of John's remains. James was able to locate his brother's remains around September 28, 1862. He then sent a telegram to his other brother Patrick, who was back home in Cleveland, from Pittsburgh. The telegram later appeared in the September 29 edition of the *Cleveland Daily Leader*. James told Patrick that he had found John's remains and would be back in Cleveland by 9:30 a.m. on September 29. "A large number of the friends of the deceased were at the depot to receive the remains," the *Daily Leader* published in its September 30 edition. The funeral was scheduled to take place at 2:00 p.m. on Septeber 30. The rest of the paper's column on the arrival of the remains and information about the funeral services provided the reader a more thorough insight into who John Lantry really was:

> *Lieutenant Lantry was among the first who volunteered in answer to the three months' call of the president and has, we believe, been in the field during the whole war. He always stood high among the Irish portion of our citizens as a man of industry, high morality, and social virtue. He has proved his heroism upon the battlefield in an unselfish and self-sacrificing manner and leaves a name unstained by any mean act to be a household word among his patriotic countryman in our city.*

Curiously, a stone for John Lantry was erected in the National Cemetery at Antietam. You can find what may likely be a cenotaph at grave site 852.[168]

Over the course of the evening of September 17, 1862, and into the following days, the true cost of the Battle of Antietam came into focus, as officers compiled casualty lists and submitted those figures up the chain of command. Among the eight killed, fifty-nine wounded, and two missing in action in the Twenty-Third Ohio Infantry was twenty-two-year-old Charles M. Long of Poland, Ohio. Poland, a small village just outside of Youngstown and only several miles from the Pennsylvania border, had been home to the Long family for over a decade by the time Charles enlisted in the Twenty-Third Ohio in 1861. Then, with the death of their son and their inability to retrieve his remains from the Antietam battlefield, the Long family—Charles's father, John, and mother, Jemima—erected a cenotaph in honor of their son at their local house of worship, Poland Presbyterian Church. Today, the cenotaph still remains in the old graveyard located next to the church. Inscribed under Charles's name is a painful reminder of the cost of this war for the nation and the Longs: "He laid down his life for the country he loved." The loss of Charles must have been too much for his grieving parents in the coming years, with the daily reminders of his loss ever-present in Poland. By 1870, the family moved westward and settled in Kansas, where they remained on the census rolls through 1900. Charles's remains now rest inside Antietam National Cemetery, in grave site 1,344, where they were placed during the removal of the Union dead from the battlefield during the cemetery's creation.

Corporal Charles M. Long. *Courtesy of the Rutherford B. Hayes Presidential Library and Museum.*

There are many Ohioans who, today, rest in the Antietam National Cemetery who lingered between life and death in the days and weeks after the battle. Some had wounds with which little could be done with the limited medical knowledge and technology of the period and, thus, ultimately led to their death. Other wounded Ohioans were promptly removed to field hospitals and received the immediate treatment that medicine and surgeons could provide, but they still did not survive. Two soldiers of the Thirtieth Ohio Infantry illustrated this aspect of the aftermath of the Battle of Antietam.

Left: Corporal Charles M. Long, Twenty-Third Ohio Infantry. Killed in action on September 17, 1862. Grave no. 1344, Antietam National Cemetery. *Courtesy of Jon Tracey.*

Right: Cenotaph of Corporal Charles M. Long in Poland, Ohio. *Courtesy of Daniel Welch.*

John Scherlott was well above the average age of recruits and enlistees when he joined Company G of the Thirtieth Ohio on August 17, 1861. At the age of forty-three at the time of his enlistment, he served with men who were oftentimes half his age. During the afternoon attack made by the Union army's Ninth Corps, of which the Thirtieth Ohio was a part, Scherlott was severely wounded in his right leg. Not far down the line, in Company D, Edmund J. Ewers was also hit, collapsing from a mortal wound. Ewers was only nineteen years old when he enlisted on August 16, 1861, just one day before Scherlott. Both men were evacuated from the battlefield to Locust Spring or Big Spring Field Hospital. This field hospital, housed on the Geeting farm, was located off the Union army's left flank. Situated near the small hamlet of Keedysville, Maryland, it was only a few miles from the battlefield, making it a secure location to treat the wounded. Also known as Crystal Spring, the farm boasted an impressive supply of fresh water, a greatly needed resource for any field hospital. The wounded who were taken to this field hospital were deemed to be in too fragile a condition—or wounded too seriously—to be able to travel to larger, more permanent hospital facilities

Private Edmund Ewers Jr., Thirtieth Ohio Infantry. Died on September 21, 1862. Grave no. 1364, Antietam National Cemetery. *Courtesy of Jon Tracey.*

in nearby Frederick. Both Scherlott's and Ewers's wounds were of this nature, and thus, they were taken to the Geeting farm for treatment.[169]

Edmund Ewers's wounds were of a more serious nature than Scherlott's. Edmund died just four days later, on September 21, 1862, at the age of twenty. When John Scherlott arrived at the Locust Spring Field Hospital, surgeons immediately amputated his right leg at the thigh. Few wounded soldiers who had amputations that high up on the leg and close to the trunk of the body recovered. John Scherlott died on October 20, 1862. Both men's remains were initially buried at the hospital site. As work on the newly created Antietam National Cemetery progressed during 1867, the dead who had been buried at the Locust Spring Field Hospital cemetery were reinterred in the national cemetery. Today, Edmund Ewers's remains can be found in gravesite 1,364, and just several feet away sits gravesite 1,367, the final resting place of John Scherlott. For Edmund J. Ewers, however, this would not be his only memorial. The people of New Lexington, Ohio—many of whom had loved ones in Company D, Thirtieth Ohio Infantry—raised, built and dedicated a monument in the town square to the company on July 4, 1876. Ewers's name can be found on its edifice.[170]

As Ohioans who had been severely wounded in the battle on the Union army's left flank south of Sharpsburg were taken to the Geeting farm for treatment, those who were wounded near the right flank were taken to the Smoketown Hospital. The hospital consumed the farms of Catherine Showman and her son, Hiram, as well as "the houses of Hoffman, Lines and Poffenberger." Over the next several days following the battle, the size of the hospital operations at Smoketown grew. Eleven doctors staffed the hospital, including B.A. Vanderkieft of the 102nd New York Infantry. In fact, it was Vanderkieft who selected the site for the hospital. "This hospital stands upon the northeast edge of the bloody field of Antietam," Indiana newspaper correspondent Lem Gentry wrote, "The site was selected by Mr. Vanderkieft on the day of the battle and was admirably chosen, being a slight elevation, descending gradually in every direction, affording good drainage and interspersed throughout with small oak and hickory trees, which give, in summer, a delightful shade." Eventually, 121 attendants; 10 ward masters; 7 washers; 31 cooks, bakers and water carriers; 4 butchers; 1 ward master-in-chief; 1 commissary sergeant; and 2 stewards staffed the field hospital. The hospital had additional help in the form of numerous women who volunteered and assisted in any way possible. One Ohioan who was taken to the Smoketown Hospital was John W. Armstrong.[171]

At the age of thirty-six, Armstrong enlisted as a private in Company B, Fifth Ohio Infantry, at the very outset of the war. Swept up, like many others, to volunteer and do his duty in the patriotic spring of 1861, John signed up for a three-month stint in the unit on April 20, 1861. With his term of service complete, he was mustered out. Just four days later, he mustered back into the Fifth Ohio, this time, for three years of service and with Company E. As the Fifth Ohio pushed toward the Dunker Church and the growing fight in the West Woods on September 17, Armstrong received a gunshot wound to the left leg. He was initially treated at a field hospital on the battlefield, where his leg was amputated, and eventually taken to the Smoketown Hospital. Sadly, the severity of his wound and the shock of the amputation was too much for his body. John Armstrong died of his wounds at Smoketown on September 24, 1862. His remains were later reinterred at grave site 1,345 in the national cemetery.[172]

Another soldier of the Fifth Ohio who was wounded in the fighting around the Dunker Church was George W. Gentle. Born in 1839 in Hancock County, Illinois, George Gentle, like John Armstrong, enlisted in the Fifth Ohio, Company E, in the wake of the attack on Fort Sumter in April 1861. He, too, answered the call for three months' service and mustered out at his term's conclusion on June 19. Gentle immediately reenlisted that same day into the same company, this time, as one of its corporals. It was not long into their fight near the Dunker Church that Gentle was wounded by a gunshot through his right thigh. "The ball entered to the outside of the right pyramidalis muscle, passed outward and downward in front of the femur, and emerged at a spot in the integument corresponding to the insertion in the gluteus maximus," wrote Assistant Surgeon J.H. Bill. Gentle was initially treated at a field hospital following his wounding, but the Buckeye was later transferred to U.S. Army General Hospital No. 3 in Frederick on October 1. During the initial examination of Gentle's wound at the hospital in

Private George W. Gentle, Fifth Ohio Infantry. Killed in action on September 17, 1862. Grave no. 1480, Antietam National Cemetery. *Courtesy of Jon Tracey.*

Frederick, Surgeon Bill noted that it was not an "injury of a grave character" or even suspected to be.[173]

Just three weeks later, however, Gentle's wound and his health took a turn for the worse. Surgeon Bill wrote in his case report of Gentle's treatment that on October 23, "a hemorrhage from both wounds took place." Although the wound was packed to stop the hemorrhage, no further treatment was given. Just two days later, Gentle hemorrhaged again. While working to stop it, surgeons noticed that his thigh and hip were very swollen, abscesses were present and more hemorrhaging was found, as well as an ulceration of one of the vessels in the leg. Bill immediately consulted with another surgeon at the hospital. Surgeon H.S. Hewitt, along with Bill, suggested to Gentle that a procedure be done to correct some of these recent developments in his wounds. Gentle demurred, pushing off any kind of surgery. Four days later, the hemorrhaging returned. This time, Gentle requested the surgery to tie off the artery in his leg. The procedure went forward. Although the surgeons were able to find and tie off the external iliac, they did not have time to find the "bleeding vessel," as, "at this stage of the operation, the shock to the patient was so severe that it was necessary to finish all operative interference as soon as possible." Gentle died just twenty-four hours later on October 28, 1862. The two surgeons performed an autopsy and searched for the "bleeding vessel" that they were unable to find during the operation. Both believed this to be the cause of death. Despite an extensive search, neither were able to find it. Both surgeons felt the surgery was the best course of action for Gentle, but unfortunately, they were unable to save him. Today, Gentle rests in grave 1,480 in Antietam National Cemetery.[174]

These stories are just some of the more than twenty-three thousand individual stories of the casualties at Antietam, and they only highlight the experiences of one state's soldiers. Despite the passage of time, if we listen closely, their stories still have much to tell.

OHIO BURIALS IN THE ANTIETAM NATIONAL CEMETERY

Name	Rank	Unit	Company	Grave No.	
Lucas, Elisha	private	Fourth Ohio Infantry	Company B	1482	
Walduck, John	private	Fourth Ohio Infantry	Company E	1485	
Wellchance, Layfayette	private	Fourth Ohio Infantry	Company K	1487	
Wise, Demas C.	private	Fourth Ohio Infantry	Company I	1486	
Armstrong, John W.	private	Fifth Ohio Infantry	Company E	1345	
Fitzgibbons, Patrick	corporal	Fifth Ohio Infantry	Company I	1341	
Gentle, George W.	corporal	Fifth Ohio Infantry	Company E	1480	
Gutzler, Jacob	private	Fifth Ohio Infantry	Company A	1348	
Howard, George	private	Fifth Ohio Infantry	Company B	1369	
Jobenour, L.	private	Fifth Ohio Infantry		1397	
Kendall, Lorenzo	private	Fifth Ohio Infantry	Company K	1352	
Miller, John M.	private	Fifth Ohio Infantry	Company F	1354	
Spellman, William	private	Fifth Ohio Infantry	Company E	1347	
Bacon, Henry	private	Seventh Ohio Infantry	Company H	1350	
Coe, Allison	private	Seventh Ohio Infantry	Company G	1373	

Notes
Frederick, Antietam, died, December 4, 1862.
Frederick, Antietam, died, November 26, 1862.
Frederick, Antietam, died, November 16, 1862.
Frederick, Antietam, died, December 12, 1862.
Wounded in action at Antietam, September 17, 1862. Died of wounds, September 24, 1862.
Wounded in action at Antietam, September 17, 1862. Died of wounds, October 1, 1862.
Wounded in action at Antietam, September 17, 1862. Died of complications from his wound, October 28, 1862.
Killed in action at Antietam, September 17, 1862.
Wounded in action at Antietam, September 17, 1862. Died of wounds, September 21, 1862.
Middletown
Killed in action at Antietam, September 17, 1862.
Killed in action at Antietam, September 17, 1862.
Killed in action at Antietam, September 17, 1862.
Killed in action at Antietam, September 17, 1862.
Wounded in action at Antietam, September 17, 1862. Died of wounds, September 21, 1862.

Name	Rank	Unit	Company	Grave No.
Everett, David	private	Seventh Ohio Infantry	Company E	1375
Goodsell, Edward W.	corporal	Seventh Ohio Infantry	Company C	1374
Kanas, James P.	private	Seventh Ohio Infantry		1244
McFadden, John	private	Seventh Ohio Infantry	Company I	1481
Meacham, Eldridge F.	private	Seventh Ohio Infantry	Company B	1351
Sperick, George O.	private	Seventh Ohio Infantry	Company B	1353
Basler, Jonas	sergeant	Eighth Ohio Infantry	Company F	1500
Boughton, Charles W.	corporal	Eighth Ohio Infantry	Company H	1357
Briggs, John	sergeant	Eighth Ohio Infantry	Company D	1340
Cole, Orville B.	private	Eighth Ohio Infantry	Company G	1332
Conner, John M.	private	Eighth Ohio Infantry	Company E	1356
Fields, John S.	private	Eighth Ohio Infantry	Company F	1334
Keesan, John		Eighth Ohio Infantry	Company G	1333
Lantry, John	lieutenant	Eighth Ohio Infantry	Company B	852
Mann, William Riley	private	Eighth Ohio Infantry	Company H	1483
Newell, Dawin D.	private	Eighth Ohio Infantry	Company K	1495
Nichols, Frederick E.	musician	Eighth Ohio Infantry	Company C	1355

Notes
Wounded in action at Antietam, September 17, 1862. Died of wounds, October 6, 1862.
Wounded in action at Antietam, September 17, 1862. Died of wounds, September 19, 1862.
Cumberland
Died of consumption, October 31, 1862.
Killed in action at Antietam, September 17, 1862.
Killed in action at Antietam, September 17, 1862.
Wounded in action at Antietam, September 17, 1862. Died of wounds, October 6, 1862.
Wounded in action at Antietam, September 17, 1862. Died of wounds, September 21, 1862.
Killed in action at Antietam, September 17, 1862.
Killed in action at Antietam, September 17, 1862.
Wounded in action at Antietam, September 17, 1862. Died of wounds, September 24, 1862.
Killed in action at Antietam, September 17, 1862.
Killed in action at Antietam, September 17, 1862.
Killed in action at Antietam, September 17, 1862.
Died of diarrhea, November 30, 1862.
Wounded in action at Antietam, September 17, 1862. Died of wounds, September 25, 1862.
Killed in action at Antietam, September 17, 1862.

Name	Rank	Unit	Company	Grave No.
Palmerton, William S.	private	Eighth Ohio Infantry	Company F	1336
Richardson, William P.	private	Eighth Ohio Infantry	Company A	1339
Trube, Franklin	private	Eighth Ohio Infantry	Company E	1337
West, Albert	sergeant	Eighth Ohio Infantry	Company H	1335
Zongker, David	private	Eighth Ohio Infantry	Company A	1338
Baker, John	private	Eleventh Ohio Infantry	Company E	1420
Debretz, Michael	corporal	Eleventh Ohio Infantry	Company K	1421
Ferry, Amos	private	Eleventh Ohio Infantry	Company E	1366
McCreara, James	private	Eleventh Ohio Infantry	Company C	1414
Schlasser, John	private	Eleventh Ohio Infantry	Company K	1415
Tapley, George S.	corporal	Eleventh Ohio Infantry	Company B	1419
Weiner, John	private	Eleventh Ohio Infantry	Company K	1329
Brooks, Jonas	private	Twelfth Ohio Infantry	Company I	1416
Cockerell, William A.	private	Twelfth Ohio Infantry	Company C	1413
Goodloe, Vivian	corporal	Twelfth Ohio Infantry	Company C	1327
Light, Henry C.	private	Twelfth Ohio Infantry	Company I	1399
Reichman, Jacob	private	Twelfth Ohio Infantry	Company H	1362

Notes
Killed in action at Antietam, September 17, 1862.
Killed in action at Antietam, September 17, 1862.
Killed in action at Antietam, September 17, 1862.
Killed in action at Antietam, September 17, 1862.
Killed in action at Antietam, September 17, 1862.
Killed in action at South Mountain, September 14, 1862.
Killed in action at South Mountain, September 14, 1862.
Killed in action at Antietam, September 17, 1862.
Killed in action at South Mountain, September 14, 1862.
Killed in action at Antietam, September 17, 1862.
Wounded in action at South Mountain. Date of death unknown.
Killed in action at Antietam, September 17, 1862.
Killed in action at Fox's Gap, September 14, 1862.
Killed in action at Fox's Gap, September 14, 1862.
Killed in action at Antietam, September 17, 1862.
Middletown
Wounded in action at Antietam, September 17, 1862. Died of wounds, September 19, 1862.

Name	Rank	Unit	Company	Grave No.
Sherron (Sherrow), Laban	private	Twelfth Ohio Infantry	Company I	1363
Went, Lewis	private	Twelfth Ohio Infantry	Company C	1365
Armstrong, Joshua A.	sergeant	Twenty-Third Ohio Infantry	Company F	1326
Barnes, Joshua L.	private	Twenty-Third Ohio Infantry	Company A	1402
Bollinger, Jacob	private	Twenty-Third Ohio Infantry	Company K	1405
Brookman, Charles V.	private	Twenty-Third Ohio Infantry	Company C	1404
Detrick, George W.	private	Twenty-Third Ohio Infantry	Company F	1409
Dixon, Robert A.	private	Twenty-Third Ohio Infantry	Company I	1434
Dunn, John	private	Twenty-Third Ohio Infantry	Company A	1437
Edwards, William	private	Twenty-Third Ohio Infantry	Company F	1401
Eldridge, James V.	private	Twenty-Third Ohio Infantry	Company D	1360
Goodman, Mabery	private	Twenty-Third Ohio Infantry	Company E	1324
Harper, Wilson B.	private	Twenty-Third Ohio Infantry	Company H	1400
Lindley, John H.	sergeant	Twenty-Third Ohio Infantry	Company D	1406
Long, Charles M.	corporal	Twenty-Third Ohio Infantry	Company E	1344
Parsons, Henry W.	private	Twenty-Third Ohio Infantry	Company H	1498
Richardson, David I.	private	Twenty-Third Ohio Infantry	Company H	1407

Notes
Antietam
Wounded in action at Antietam, September 17, 1862. Died of wounds, September 21, 1862.
Killed in action at Antietam, September 17, 1862.
Killed in action at Fox's Gap, September 14, 1862.
Wounded in action at Antietam, September 17, 1862. Died of wounds, September 25, 1862.
Wounded in action at South Mountain, September 14, 1862. Died of wounds, September 22, 1862.
Killed in action at Fox's Gap, September 14, 1862.
Wounded in action at South Mountain, September 14, 1862. Died of wounds, September 15, 1862.
Killed in action at South Mountain, September 14, 1862.
Killed in action at South Mountain, September 14, 1862.
Wounded in action at Antietam, September 17, 1862. Died of wounds, October 6, 1862.
Killed in action at Antietam, September 17, 1862.
Wounded in action at South Mountain, September 14, 1862. Died of wounds, September 17, 1862.
Wounded in action at South Mountain, September 14, 1862. Died of wounds, October 3, 1862.
Killed in action at Antietam, September 17, 1862.
Wounded in action at South Mountain, September 14, 1862. Died of wounds October 6, 1862.
Wounded in action at South Mountain, September 14, 1862. Died of wounds, September 27, 1862.

Name	Rank	Unit	Company	Grave No.
Smith, Benjamin H.	private	Twenty-Third Ohio Infantry	Company F	1265
Spain, David R.	private	Twenty-Third Ohio Infantry	Company F	1330
Wagner, Joseph	private	Twenty-Third Ohio Infantry	Company K	1325
Pierce, Sylvester	private	Twenty-Ninth Ohio Infantry	Company K	1478
Allton, James E.	private	Thirtieth Ohio Infantry	Company D	1379
Ewers, Edmund J.	private	Thirtieth Ohio Infantry	Company D	1364
Jadwin, Isaac	private	Thirtieth Ohio Infantry	Company D	1412
Noble, John	private	Thirtieth Ohio Infantry	Company D	1499
Noble, William	private	Thirtieth Ohio Infantry	Company D	1403
Scherlott, John	private	Thirtieth Ohio Infantry	Company G	1367
S., T.	private	Thirtieth Ohio Infantry		1424
Taylor, David	corporal	Thirtieth Ohio Infantry	Company I	1361
Wolfe, Henry F.	sergeant	Thirtieth Ohio Infantry	Company A	1359
Anderson, John	private	Thirty-Sixth Ohio Infantry	Company K	1428
Cherington, Spencer	private	Thirty-Sixth Ohio Infantry	Company K	1496
Daley, Andrew J.	private	Thirty-Sixth Ohio Infantry	Company K	1431
Gibbons, Henry J.	private	Thirty-Sixth Ohio Infantry	Company G	1432

Notes
Killed in action at South Mountain, September 14, 1862.
Killed in action at Antietam, September 17, 1862.
Killed in action at Antietam, September 17, 1862.
U.S. Army Hospital, Frederick. Died of disease, October 20, 1862.
Killed in action at Fox's Gap, September 14, 1862.
Wounded in action at Antietam, September 17, 1862. Died of wounds, September 21, 1862.
Killed in action at Fox's Gap, September 14, 1862.
Wounded in action at South Mountain, September 14, 1862. Died of infection, October 15, 1862.
Wounded in action at South Mountain, September 14, 1862. Died of wounds October 11, 1862.
Wounded in action at Antietam, September 17, 1862. Died of wounds October 20, 1862.
South Mountain
Killed in action at Antietam, September 16, 1862.
Wounded in action at Antietam, September 17, 1862. Died of wounds, September 21, 1862.
Killed in action at South Mountain, September 14, 1862.
Killed in action at Fox's Gap, September 14, 1862.
Killed in action at South Mountain, September 14, 1862.
Killed in action at South Mountain, September 14, 1862.

Name	Rank	Unit	Company	Grave No.	
Hoover, John W.	private	Thirty-Sixth Ohio Infantry	Company K	1497	
McClane, Edward B.	private	Thirty-Sixth Ohio Infantry	Company B	1473	
Rice, William	private	Thirty-Sixth Ohio Infantry	Company K	1448	
Kohler, John J.	private	Sixty-Sixth Ohio Infantry	Company I	1372	
Mowser, Casper	private	Sixty-Sixth Ohio Infantry	Company G	1371	
Morris, William Edward	private	Sixty-Sixth Ohio Infantry	Company I	1368	
Buckley, John	private	Eighty-Seventh Ohio Infantry	Company C	1493	
Miller, John R.	corporal	Eighty-Seventh Ohio Infantry	Company D	1263	
Ball, John	private	First Ohio Light Artillery	Battery L	1376	
Kennedy, Ira	private	First Ohio Battery		1472	

Notes
Wounded in action at Fox's Gap, September 14, 1862. Died of wounds, October 6, 1862.
Died of disease, October 13, 1862.
Wounded in action at South Mountain, September 14, 1862. Died of wounds, September 15, 1862.
Wounded in action at Antietam, September 17, 1862. Died of wounds, October 14, 1862.
Wounded in action at Antietam, September 17, 1862. Died of wounds, October 10, 1862.
Wounded in action at Antietam, September 17, 1862. Died of wounds, September 21, 1862.
Frederick, Antietam, died September 25, 1862
Frederick, Antietam, died September 19, 1862.
Died of illness, September 26, 1862.
Died October 6, 1862.

8

OHIOANS REMEMBER AMERICA'S
BLOODIEST DAY

*I deem it a duty for every active participant in important events of the Civil War
to put on record what he remembers that may be of value to the future historians
of that struggle.*[175]
—Thomas F. Galwey, Eighth Ohio Volunteer Infantry

Read before the Commandery of the Military Order of the Loyal Legion
of the United States on December 1, 1897, Galwey began his address
by imploring those in attendance to preserve their memories of the events of
September 17, 1862. Indeed, in the thirty-five years after the battle had ended,
Galwey and the numerous other Buckeyes who saw combat at Antietam did
just that. Some wrote letters home to loved ones and friends in the days after
the battle, while others wrote letters to the editors of their hometown Ohio
newspapers. Men also wrote in private journals and diaries. Commanders
filed official reports of the Ohio units that fought that day. But for the longer
memory of the Ohioans' actions and sacrifices on the fields of Sharpsburg,
Maryland, private diaries, letters and hard-to-access government reports
were simply not enough. In the decades following the war, the fields of
battle were preserved as eternal hallowed grounds for future generations to
visit. Dotting many of these former battlefield landscapes were monuments
erected by veterans, veterans' organizations and state commissions, all in an
effort to preserve the memory of those who had given "their last full measure
of devotion." The state of Ohio was no different than many others in their
efforts to remember the fields where so many of its native sons had spilled
blood, died or had their lives forever changed.

In May and October 1902, the General Assembly of Ohio passed legislation that created the Ohio Antietam Battlefield Commission. The commission was "charged with the duty of erecting suitable monuments to mark the positions of Ohio troops on the battlefield…and to mark the place where Commissary Sergeant William McKinley issued rations to his regiment." The commission was tasked with purchasing the land where the Ohio units "advanced" on September 17, and in addition to financial rules and regulations, it was also instructed to work with "the representatives of regiments and of said battery…as to the style of monuments they desire and as to the inscription to be put thereon." Those men who had fought forty years earlier then had, at Ohio's expense, the opportunity to ensure their actions and losses would be remembered forever. Before the work began, the governor of Ohio George K. Nash appointed members to the commission in June 1902. The commission consisted largely of veterans of the battle, including Majors David Cunningham and J.T. Moore, Thirtieth Ohio; T.J. West, W.W. Miller and E.T. Naylor, Eighth Ohio; and D.H. Kimberly, Twenty-Third Ohio. The commission wasted no time in getting to work on preserving the legacy of these men and units.[176]

Just two months after they were appointed, in August 1902, the commission's members met in Keedysville, Maryland, and began locating sites for all of the monuments that were to be erected. The only plats of ground they had to purchase were for the Eleventh Ohio monument; the Fifth, Seventh and Sixty-Sixth Ohio Regiments' combined monument; and the McKinley monument. "The other monuments were located on the public avenues and roads." They also decided that the monuments were to be made of Westerly, Quincy or Barre granite, requests for which were sent to Ohio, New York and New England granite companies. After a year and a half of work, the commission was ready to unveil and dedicate these stone memorials on the battlefield.[177]

The unveiling date originally selected by the commission was to be the forty-first anniversary of the battle, September 17, 1903. This was not to be. There was great anxiety that the totality of the work on all the monuments on the battlefield would not be completed in time, and further still, the state of New Jersey had already selected that date to unveil and dedicate its monuments. Thus, the commission selected October 13, 1903 as the new date. It turned out to be an idyllic day for the Ohio commission. As the day began, it became quickly apparent that there would be a large turnout for the dedication of these monuments to the brave Ohioans who fought during the war's bloodiest day. Several hundred veterans returned to the battlefield that day, as well as several hundred citizens of the Buckeye State. In addition to this large gathering, the day's ceremonies included many noted and influential leaders either in the crowd or among the commission during the dedications. These individuals included Governor Nash, acting secretary of war General Robert Shaw Oliver, General Ezra Carman of the Antietam Battlefield Board and General Ian Hamilton of the British Army. The only notable attendee who was unable to be there due to a rigorous schedule of engagements was President Theodore Roosevelt. The crowd slowly made its way to the "now-historic Dunker Church, baptized during the battle with the best blood of both armies," the location for the services that were to be held that day. At 10:00 a.m., the dedication of Ohio's monuments on the battlefield of Antietam began.[178]

Major David Cunningham, Thirtieth Ohio Infantry, began the ceremony with the introduction of Reverend O.S. Kriebel. Speaking on the importance of their memory for current and future generations, the reverend, in his prayer that morning, told the crowd, with heads bowed, "May the memory of those who have freely offered themselves upon their country's altar be a cherished heritage and a source of living inspiration to the millions who are enjoying the unnumbered blessing of our blood-bought institutions." At the conclusion of the prayer, Cunningham, the chairman of the commission, introduced Captain W.W. Miller of the Eighth Ohio. As secretary, he gave those in attendance a brief report of the activities of the Ohio Antietam Battlefield Commission over the past year. Then it was time for Chairman Cunningham to provide some introductory remarks before the commission presented the monuments to Governor Nash. He, too, spoke on the importance of the memories of these events lasting into the future through the placement of these monuments. "Not that these monuments can add new luster to their fame; that is not their purpose," Cunningham said. Rather, they are "for the further purpose of enabling the descendants and friends of the men who fought here, when, in the years to come, they may visit this field, to find the exact spot where their ancestors fought and maybe died." At the conclusion of his remarks, Cunningham introduced Ohio governor Nash.[179]

The governor spoke on many themes associated with the day, including the memory of those events. He took time to address the forty years that had progressed since that day, the hope of Lincoln that, one day, we will be "the better angels of our nature." Nash recalled the actions of William McKinley, the soldier; the value of loving the flag; and the importance of defending the government. He even spoke of the unity the country expressed in the late Spanish-American War and of the sacrifice of both Northern and Southern sons in a common effort. Nash then presented to the acting secretary of war these monuments for their "care and keeping of your [War] Department." Nash said he did "this with great pleasure, because I know that our government will forever cherish and preserve them for the benefit of future generations." Brief words from the acting secretary and Cunningham transitioned the ceremony to the main orator of the day, General R.P. Kennedy. He, too, stressed the importance of remembering the date September 17, 1862, and those that participated in the battle and their sacrifice. "We must not forget the cost at which all these [glory and liberty] have been purchased, nor the sacrifices necessary to win them," Kennedy intoned. He continued, "We must not forget the great leaders who, here, offered up their lives and the heroic men whose names are written in the records of their country's history." Moments later, after reminiscences about the battle as a whole, the Emancipation Proclamation and the importance of President Abraham Lincoln to the Union war effort, Kennedy looked across the crowd of veterans and their family and friends and addressed the reason for their gathering that day: Ohio's role at the Battle of Antietam.[180]

"On this battlefield, Ohio found her place," Kennedy began on the topic. "We lift these monuments not alone to the dead but to the living; they bear witness to coming generations of the valor of the fathers who preserve our institutions for the sons who were to come after." Of those fathers to which he referred, he asked, "What deeds of heroism were here enacted?" He recalled, "Colonel Coleman of the Eleventh, charging the bridge only to fall in the very moment of victory," and "Colonel Clark [*sic*] of the Thirty-Sixth, leading his men across plowed fields and fallow, in the grand charge, only to fall in the front rank of the peril." Although Kennedy went on to explore many other themes, his remarks about the monuments to these Ohioans at Antietam struck "the mystic chords of memory" among those veterans of the battle in attendance.

It seems to be eminently proper that the State of Ohio should not only erect and dediate monuments upon this field to commemorate the achievements of the regiments and commands from that state and so mark for all time the points where her sons did battle, but it is equally fitting that it should erect a monument to mark the spot where one of her younger soldiers, in the performance of his duty, contributed to the comfort and added to the strength and courage of that army.…Their names will go on down the centuries as the martyrs of the Republic.

The dedication ceremony continued. British general Hamilton was recognized, saying just a few words before Chairman Cunningham introduced General Eugene Powell, who commanded the Sixty-Sixth Ohio Infantry during the Battle of Antietam. Powell was scheduled as the second orator of the ceremony. Speaking to his fellow veterans of the battle in the audience, Powell noted that, like him, they, too, had "just taken part in the dedication of monuments in memory of your dead who fell here." Powell hoped that these monuments, in honor of the Ohioans living and dead, would not only "stand while this Union exists," but also have

Brt. Brig. Gen. E. POWELL
Col, 193d Ohio Inf.

Lieutenant Colonel Eugene Powell. *Courtesy of the MOLLUS Collection, United States Army Heritage and Education Center, Carlisle, Pennsylvania.*

"succeeding generations catch inspiration as they look upon these statues erected here; may they thereby increase their love of country, renew and reiterate their pledges of loyalty and devotion to this Republic as they gaze upon these images in bronze, marble and granite of your fallen heroes, standing, as they do, in mute but sublime silence all over these fair fields and upon the sides and tops of these hills."[181]

Following a reading of the report that was filed after the battle of Lieutenant Colonel Hector Tyndale's brigade, the ceremony moved toward its conclusion. Each final speaker that day opined on the need for all present and future generations not yet born to remember these men, these Buckeyes. John Finn of the Eighth Ohio Infantry assured those in attendance that the names and actions of the Ohioans at Antietam would never be forgotten, as they would be found "in the archives of the great State of Ohio, and, as well, in the archives of the government at the capital of the nation, where it will be preserved forever and ever." Powell, in his closing remarks, agreed with Finn. He stated that the monuments that had been built would be a "a record of your heroism [and] will thus be preserved and handed down from age to age."[182]

The soldiers from Ohio who participated in America's single bloodiest day at the Battle of Antietam immediately recorded their memories of the battle. In the days, weeks and months after the battle, they wrote letters home to friends and family, sharing their experiences. They wrote letters to editors of various newspapers. These men also wrote down their experiences at Antietam in journals and diaries. But these memories were quickly forgotten as the war progressed; more battles were waged, and more Ohioans were lost. Newspapers carried the most recent news from the front, and those back home who received letters from loved ones in these units spoke of Fredericksburg, Gettysburg and many other engagements—not Antietam. During the postwar years, their memories were again put to paper in publications by and for veterans. They made speeches about their experiences at Antietam and recalled the names of their comrades who had given their all on that battlefield. Those who had worked so hard on the Ohio Antietam Battlefield Commission to bring these monuments to fruition felt this was the best way—the longest-lasting way—to remember the actions of the Ohio soldiers and units at Antietam, a more tangible link than lost newspaper editions and vaulted reports in the nation's capital. Chaplain W.R. Parsons, who ended the ceremony with a prayer before the day's crowd walked the field and inspected the monuments, agreed. "These monuments, which loving hands have erected to the memory of our brave comrades, will ever bear witness to their patriotism and loyalty," he preached. "Their glory shall endure forever and go with America's drumbeat around the world and spread everywhere the gospel of liberty and of God."[183]

CONCLUSION

Nimrod Burke moved to Ohio as a free African American man in 1854. He was born free in Virginia on the outskirts of the future Manassas battlefield. Once he arrived in the Buckeye State, Nimrod went to work. He found employment "as a handyman" with Melvin Clarke in Marietta. Clarke grew to trust and respect Burke and taught him to read, write and count. Nimrod was married in 1860, but when war gripped the torn nation, Nimrod attempted to give up his freedom and family to fight for the United States. But because of his race, he was denied.

When Clarke helped raise the Thirty-Sixth Ohio Infantry, he brought Burke along as a teamster and scout. Nimrod served with Clarke's command throughout the campaigns in western Virginia and in the Maryland Campaign as well. In these conflicts, Clarke, Nimrod's educator, employer and acquaintance, fell in action. Because of Clarke's abolitionist views, he likely would have been pleased that the federal victory in the campaign prompted President Abraham Lincoln to announce the preliminary Emancipation Proclamation five days after the bloodiest day in American military history.[184]

Lincoln signed the final Emancipation Proclamation into effect on January 1, 1863. It not only declared that enslaved persons living in the Confederacy were free, but it also allowed African American men to serve in the United States Army. Nimrod Burke eventually heeded the president's call for African American troops; in 1864, he enlisted in the Twenty-Third United States Colored Troops. Burke, who was present at Antietam, sacrificed his freedom

Above: Melvin Clarke's home in Marietta, Ohio. *Courtesy of Leight Murray.*

Left: Melvin Clarke's grave in Marietta, Ohio, notes his death at Antietam. *Courtesy of Leight Murray.*

Opposite: Officers of His Regiment and His Associates of the Bar of Marietta erected this obelisk over Clarke's grave in his memory. *Courtesy of Leight Murray.*

to preserve it for four million others, ensuring that Melvin Clarke did not die in vain on the battlefield that made emancipation a viable condition of a Union victory in the Civil War.[185]

The Ohioans who fought at Antietam praised Lincoln's measure more than those who condemned it; 81 percent of the Ohio's counties that supplied troops who fought at Antietam voted for Lincoln in the election of 1860.

"You will like the president's proclamation," Rutherford Hayes wrote home. "I am not sure about it but am content." This feeling likely summed up those of many Buckeye staters regarding the Emancipation Proclamation.[186]

In September 1862, 876 Ohioans became casualties of war in western Maryland, which represent just over 5 percent of the Army of the Potomac's total force. At South Mountain, Ohio soldiers opened the action and performed well, despite the difficult terrain. On America's bloodiest day, Buckeye troops fought in the cornfield, at the Bloody Lane, over the Burnside Bridge and Antietam Creek and south of Sharpsburg.[187]

Regarding the outcome of the campaign, Ohio's soldiers believed it ended in their favor. "It has been the hardest battle fought during the war, and the Rebels were beaten," said Private John Kenney of the Eleventh Ohio. The Twenty-Third Ohio's Charles Hay told his hometown readers, "The results of the late contest are unquestionably victory to the national arms, and rout, ruin and panic to the vile hosts of Jeff Davis." Surgeon Thomas Ebright wanted to ensure that the readers of the *Holmes County Farmer* knew the campaign was a success. "It was a victory, though dearly purchased, and by it, I think the Union is saved," he began. Ebright recognized the importance of September 1862 for future generations. "If ever there could be in one's existence a day longer to be remembered than another, let that day be when the Rebel hosts discomfited and panic-stricken, driven from the shores of Maryland, with the anathemas of loyal men ringing in accord with the music of the national artillery heralding their departure."[188]

Ohio's soldiers played a key role in preserving the Union with their actions at South Mountain and Antietam. While many of these men rest on the field they won, survivors, such as Rutherford Hayes and William McKinley, continued to serve the country they fought so dearly to keep on the hills and fields of Maryland in September 1862.

Appendix

WILLIAM MCKINLEY, ANTIETAM'S ONLY FUTURE PRESIDENT

William McKinley was an Ohioan through-and-through. Although his early years saw him and his family move several times, they never strayed from the Western Reserve, and when the war broke out in 1861, McKinley joined the army and left for the front from a small village near the Pennsylvania border: Poland, Ohio. Located approximately seven miles southeast of Youngstown, Poland has a long history. In 1796, it became the first charted township in the Western Reserve. Within six years, the village of Poland was founded. As the village and township became a part of the newly formed state of Ohio in 1803, infrastructure within the community, as well as locally, expanded rapidly.

The residents of Poland then, as well as today, firmly believed in a great education for their children. By 1830, Poland Academy was opened by a local Presbyterian minister. Although it went through several name changes, as well as locations and headmasters, Poland Academy, later Poland Seminary, a private institution, remains a staple in the community as Poland Seminary High School. One student who matriculated through this institution was future president William McKinley. Originally from Niles, Ohio, in Trumbull County to the north, McKinley's family moved to Poland in 1852 to provide their children with a better education than what could be found in Niles. Young William graduated from the town's educational institution in 1859 and moved on to higher education at both Mount Union College in Alliance, Ohio, and Allegheny College in Meadville, Pennsylvania. Unfortunately, due to poor health and possibly depression, William returned home and did not graduate from either university.

As war descended and the country fractured, McKinley, along with thousands of other boys his age, enlisted into military service. War rallies, patriotic speeches and even drilling on the green in Poland began just days after the surrender of Fort Sumter and President Lincoln's call for volunteers. McKinley, however, was hesitant at first. As men from Poland and nearby Lowellville organized and drilled, young Will "decided to wait and study the situation a little more carefully at first. I wanted to see how the boys lived in camp and wished to understand myself so thoroughly that I would not regret any action that I decided to take."[189]

The newly formed companies left for Columbus to be mustered into federal service. It was during this time, early June 1861, that McKinley, as well as his cousin William McKinley Osborne, decided to enlist. According to local history, it was at the Sparrow House, a local tavern, that McKinley enlisted in the army. One history of the village notes, "It was on the porch of this tavern that William McKinley enlisted in the Union army in 1861." Yet, other accounts say that it was not at the Sparrow House where this meaningful step in McKinley's life took place. Osborne, later in life, recorded the moment:

> There was great excitement at that time, and hundreds of people followed the soldiers. Will and I were among them. We drove in a buggy over to Youngstown, and there saw the company leave for Columbus. On our way back to Poland that night, we discussed the matter together and decided that it was our duty to volunteer, and we thought that the men who staid [sic] would be despised by the community.
>
> When we reached home, Will told his mother what we had concluded to do, and she, at once, replied, "Well, boys, if you think it is your duty to fight for your country, I think you ought to go." A few days after this, I left Poland for home and told father that I wanted to go to the army. I knew he would allow me to go, as Aunt Nancy advised. I was not disappointed. My father was a Democrat, but he was a liberal man. He told me I could do as I wished, and he gave me some money (it was gold, I remember) to fit me out. Will McKinley left Poland, and we went to Cleveland together. From there, we went to Columbus and enlisted at Camp Chase. General Fremont swore us in. Our enlistment was in cold blood and not through the enthusiasm of the moment. It was done as McKinley has done the most things of his life, as the logical offspring of careful conclusion.[190]

Whether or not McKinley signed up on the front steps or porch of the Sparrow House, it was surely a place that the future president visited and knew

William McKinley as a member of the Twenty-Third Ohio Infantry. *Courtesy of the Rutherford B. Hayes Presidential Library and Museum.*

well. It was also the site where the town sent off the recruits from Poland and Lowellville in June 1861."The balconies of the old Sparrow House (it had a double veranda then) were crowded with women, some singing, others crying. A tense and nervous strain was felt by everyone. The leading lawyer of the vicinity, Charles E. Glidden, was making a speech from the front of the tavern. As the result of his eloquence, man after man stepped up to volunteer, and as they did so, the crowd cheered, and women pinned red, white, and blue badges upon the new soldiers."[191]

McKinley's war experience, as well as his rank, progressed rapidly. Just months after enlistment, McKinley and his unit, the Twenty-Third Ohio Infantry, participated in the battle of Carnifex Ferry. Just days later, he was assigned to the brigade's quartermaster department, where he not only oversaw the continual supply of military necessities, including rations for the Twenty-Third, but where he also served as a departmental clerk. As his unit and the rest of the Kanawha Division went into winter quarters beginning in November 1861, the young soldier's duties became even greater. McKinley was then acting a commissary sergeant after the prior sergeant fell ill and was unable to perform his duties. Several months after he started this position in an acting capacity, he was finally promoted to the rank of sergeant in April 1862 at the age of nineteen. That spring and summer, McKinley and his regiment only participated in several minor affairs. Despite being called to assist Major General John Pope's army during the Second Bull Run Campaign, they did not arrive in time. For McKinley, the Twenty-Third Ohio and their brigade, their lives were about to be forever changed on September 14 at South Mountain and again on September 17 at Antietam.

The story of Commissary Sergeant William McKinley has been boiled down over the generations to the level of outright dismissal. The common phrase about his service during the battle surrounds him just serving coffee. McKinley's actions, however, were far more dangerous and heroic than common interpretations of the events relate.

September 17, 1862, began early for the men of the Twenty-Third Ohio. Moved into position at 2:00 a.m., most soldiers had not yet eaten breakfast. Many who wanted to were unable, their supply in their haversacks long since consumed. Twelve hours later, at 2:00 p.m., the Twenty-Third Ohio had yet to go into battle, although they knew it would not be long before they were ordered forward. Throughout those intervening hours, McKinley believed the men on the front line must be "faint with hunger." Sergeant McKinley sprang into action. Two miles behind the line were the wagon train and commissary stores. In the area of these stores, McKinley, "noticing some stragglers—there was plenty of them while the fight was raging...set them to work," preparing rations for the front and loading them into a wagon. He had these men prepare cooked meat, pork, beans, crackers and a barrel of hot coffee. They piled all of this into one or two wagons. McKinley could not feed his comrades without help.

Sergeant McKinley looked for volunteers to go with him on his mission. John A. Harvey of Company I, Twenty-Third Ohio, stepped forward. Harvey later recalled the harrowing ride back to the front, two miles distant.

> We started by the way of a by road through a heavy piece of woods. After driving along the road for some distance from the camp, we met an army officer with his staff and told McKinley that he must not try to go to the regiment, as it would be impossible to run the blockade, as the Rebel forces had command of an open strip in the woods. The road being so narrow that we could not turn around, Sergeant McKinley thought we had better try to go on a little farther. Before we came to the open space in the woods and close to the brow of the hill, we met another commanding officer, who ordered us to immediately turn back. We stopped and considered the matter, and the officer and his body guard went in the opposite direction. This left Sergeant McKinley to decide what was best to do. The regiment was almost in sight of us, and Sergeant McKinley was so anxious to carry out his point and give the half-starved boys something to eat. He made one more appeal to me to run the blockade; he himself risking his life in taking the lead, I following and the horses going at full speed past the blockade. We had the back end of the wagon shot away by a small cannon shot. In a very few minutes, we were safe in the midst of the half-famished regiment.[192]

Although several different versions of McKinley's actions that day appear in historiography, what happened next was witnessed by many who were in the line of the Twenty-Third Ohio. On his arrival to the front,

The monument to William McKinley stands near the spot where he performed his act on September 17, 1862. *Courtesy of the Library of Congress.*

Sergeant McKinley reported to Major James Comly, the commander of the regiment. After he reported to Comly, cheers erupted from the line as the hot rations reached the men. Numerous officers wrote on McKinley's behalf, recommending him for promotion for his brave act. Major Comly wrote to Lieutenant Colonel Rutherford Hayes, the regiment's commander who had since been transferred back to Ohio to recover from his South Mountain wound, on October 5. Comly felt McKinley "showed ability and energy of the first class in not only keeping us *fully supplied* with rations throughout the fight, but in having them fully prepared for eating also....He delivered them to us *under fire*, in two instances, with perfect method and coolness....No promotion could be made which would give more general satisfaction."[193]

McKinley continued to serve throughout the war, participating in numerous other battles, including the Battle of Cloyd's Mountain. As the war came to an end, he received a promotion to brevet major. On his return to Ohio, he began studying law. Soon, he started his practice and rose to prominence over the next decade. Also, during this time, he was married and started a family, but tragically, he lost both of his daughters at a young age. In August 1876, McKinley was nominated and later won the seat for Ohio's seventeenth congressional district. Over the next nineteen years, his star continued to rise in his new profession of politics, and he served as Ohio's governor from 1892 to 1896. On March 4, 1897, William McKinley was sworn in as the twenty-fifth president of the United States. Successfully winning a second term, he repeated the process on March 4, 1901. Tragically, on September 6, 1901, President McKinley was mortally wounded during an assassination attempt. That attempt proved successful when McKinley died from his wounds at 2:15 a.m. on September 14, 1901, ending decades of service to his country, including his heroic actions on September 17, 1862.

Notes

Introduction

1. Harper, *Ohio Handbook*, 5.
2. Ibid., 5–6.
3. Ibid., 6–7; United States War Department, *War of the Rebellion*, 1:73.
4. Harper, *Ohio Handbook*, 6–7.
5. Martin Andrews to Governor William Dennison, April 15, 1861, Governor's Official Papers, Letters Received, Ohio Historical Society; Coles, *Army*, 3.
6. Harper, *Ohio Handbook*, 9. This number was used by Whitelaw Reid, author and compiler of *Ohio in the War* (1868). This same estimate was used in official War Department records and later appeared in *Battles and Leaders of the Civil War*. Casualty figures are based on numbers in Dyer's *Compendium*, 1:16.
7. Daniel Sickles, "Address," in *In Memoriam*, 35–36.

Chapter 1

8. Williams, *1861–1865*, 340–41.
9. Lyle, *Lights and Shadows*, 107–8.
10. The Fourth Ohio was "suffering from sickness to a considerable extent," and it did not actively participate in the Maryland Campaign. Instead, it

remained in convalescent camp near Fort Gaines to recover and "recruit its strength" (Sawyer, *Military History*, 69–70; Kepler, *Service of the Fourth Regiment*, 79).; The Twenty-Ninth Ohio marched with its sister regiments to Frederick but no farther, and thus, it did not participate in the Battle of Antietam (Fritsch, *Untried Life*, 183–84).

11. Williams, *1861–1865*, 340–41.

12. September 3, 1862 entry, diary of Herbert L. Smalley, Gilder Lehrman Collection, GLC00653.14; "From the Seventh Regiment," *Western Reserve Chronicle* (Warren, OH), October 22, 1862.

13. Galwey, *Valiant Hours*, 32–33.

14. Williams, *1861–1865*, 345.

15. Ibid., 2:346; "Letters of Hayes and Crook to Cox," in Cox, *April 1861–November 1863*, 547–49.

16. "John D. Kenney to 'Friend Joe,' September 30, 1862," in "The Battles of the South Mountain and Antietam—Cox's Division," *Daily Empire* (Dayton, OH), October 17, 1862.

17. Williams, *1861–1865*, 346–49.

18. Ibid., 2:350–51.

19. Hartwig, *Antietam Creek*, 198.

20. "Kenney to 'Friend Joe,'" *Daily Empire*; "E.C. to the editors' leader, September 20, 1862," in "From Cox's Division," *Cleveland Daily Leader*, September 30, 1862.

21. Cox, *April 1861–November 1863*, 271–72; "Kenney to 'Friend Joe,'" *Daily Empire*.

22. Horton and Teverbaugh, *Eleventh Regiment*, 69–70; Hartwig, *Antietam Creek*, 199.

23. Lyle, *Lights and Shadows*, 120–21; Williams, *1861–1865*, 352.

24. Samuel W. Compton, "Autobiography," in the Samuel Wilson Compton Papers, 1840–1925, Manuscript Department, Rubenstein Library, Duke University, 91; Edward E. Schweitzer Diary, Civil War Times Illustrated Collection of Civil War Papers, United States Army Heritage and Education Center; Horton and Teverbaugh, *Eleventh Regiment*, 70.

25. Sawyer, *Military History*, 71.

26. September 13, 1862 entry, Smalley Diary.

27. Galwey, *Valiant Hours*, 35.

28. Carman, *South Mountain*, 192–94.

29. Ibid., 279–80; See Stotelmyer, *Too Useful*, 1–45, and Thorp and Rossino, *Tale Untwisted*, for more information regarding McClellan's response to the discovery of the Lost Orders.

30. Carman, *South Mountain*, 281; "Charles Hay to 'Friend Estill,' September 20, 1862," in "Army Correspondence: From Captain Drake's Company," *Holmes County Farmer* (Millersburg, OH), October 9, 1862; Cox, *April 1861–November 1863*, 274–75.

31. Lyle, *Lights and Shadows*, 123; "Hay to 'Friend Estill,'" *Holmes County Farmer*.

32. Carman, *South Mountain*, 315–17.

33. Ibid., 317; Jacob D. Cox, "Forcing Fox's and Turner's Gap," in *Battles and Leaders*, 585–86.

34. Cox, "Forcing Fox's and Turner's Gap," 2:586.

35. Lyle, *Lights and Shadows*, 124; Cox, "Forcing Fox's and Turner's Gap," 2:586; "'Watts' to Dealer, September 22, 1862," *Cleveland Plain Dealer*, September 30, 1862.

36. "E.C. to the editors' leader," *Cleveland Daily Leader*.

37. Lyle, *Lights and Shadows*, 126–27.

38. Cox, "Forcing Fox's and Turner's Gap," 2:587; Carman, *South Mountain*, 319.

39. "Hay to 'Friend Estill,'" *Holmes County Farmer*; Williams, *1861–1865*, 355; Carman, *South Mountain*, 324.

40. Williams, *1861–1865*, 355; "Hay to 'Friend Estill,'" *Holmes County Farmer*.

41. Carman, *South Mountain*, 324.

42. Williams, *1861–1865*, 356–57.

43. Carman, *South Mountain*, 325; Compton, "Autobiography," 93–94; Ward, *Twelfth Ohio*, 58.

44. Carman, *South Mountain*, 325–27; United States War Department, *War of the Rebellion*, 19:469.

45. United States War Department, *War of the Rebellion*, 19:459, 463–64; Johnson and Anderson, *Artillery Hell*, 79; Carman, *South Mountain*, 326–27.

46. Hoptak, *Battle*, 54–55.

47. Cox, "Forcing Fox's and Turner's Gap," 2:587.

48. "'Philo' to 'Ed. Register,' September 22, 1862," in "Army Correspondence," *Mahoning Register*, October 9, 1862, a copy is in Twenty-Third Ohio Infantry File, Antietam National Battlefield Library; Carman, *South Mountain*, 327; Hayes memoir, Box 10, Folder 23, Ezra Carman Papers, Manuscripts and Archives Division, MSS-473, New York Public Library; Lyle, *Lights and Shadows*, 129.

49. Hoptak, *Battle*, 56; Lyle, *Lights and Shadows*, 130; Horton and Teverbaugh, *Eleventh Regiment*, 72.

50. Beyer and Keydel, *Deeds of Valor*, 72–73.

51. Compton, "Autobiography," 94; "'Philo' to 'Ed. Register,'" *Mahoning Register*.

52. Carman, *South Mountain*, 328–29.

53. Horton and Teverbaugh, *Eleventh Regiment*, 72.
54. "Kenney to 'Friend Joe,'" *Daily Empire*; *Mahoning Register* clipping, September 25, 1862, Eleventh Ohio Infantry File, Antietam National Battlefield Library.
55. Hoptak, *Battle*, 61.
56. Cox, "Forcing Fox's and Turner's Gap," 2:587.
57. Ibid., 2:587–89.
58. Hugh Ewing, U.S. Army Generals' Report of Civil War Service, roll 3, M1098, RG 94, National Archives; Hoptak, *Battle*, 82–84; Cox, *April 1861–November 1863*, 285.
59. Compton, "Autobiography," 95; "'Watts,'" *Cleveland Plain Dealer*; Horton and Teverbaugh, *Eleventh Regiment*, 72.
60. Alexander Wight to Brother, September 26, 1862, Twenty-Third Ohio Infantry File, Antietam National Battlefield Library.
61. Ibid.; Williams, *1861–1865*, 357.
62. "Hayes at Middletown," *New York Herald*, April 9, 1877; Card, "Hayes' Visit," 144; Williams, *1861–1865*, 360.
63. "Hayes," *New York Herald*.
64. "Wounded at South Mountain," *Herald and Torch Light* (Hagerstown, MD), June 28, 1876.
65. Card, "Hayes' Visit,"144; "Hayes," *New York Herald*.
66. "Frederick A. Seymour to Editor, October 13, 1862," in Staats, *Seventh Ohio*, 87.
67. Carman, *South Mountain*, 371.
68. Ibid.; Ray, "Journal," 64.
69. Galwey, *Valiant Hours*, 35–36. The Second Corps's strength on September 17 was 16,065 men. Sawyer simply overestimated the number of soldiers in the corps (Sawyer, *Military History*, 72; Carman, *Antietam*, 576).
70. Sawyer, *Military History*, 73–74.

Chapter 2

71. Staats, *Seventh Ohio*, 87; Ray, "Journal," 64; September 15, 1862 entry, Smalley Diary.
72. September 15, 1862 entry, Smalley Diary; Staats, *Seventh Ohio*, 87–88.
73. Staats, *Seventh Ohio*, 88; "Seventh Regiment," *Western Reserve Chronicle* (Warren, OH); September 15, 1862 entry, Smalley Diary.
74. Staats, *Seventh Ohio*, 88; September 15–16, 1862 entries, Smalley Diary; Ray, "Journal," 65.

75. Staats, *Seventh Ohio*, 88; September 16, 1862 entry, Smalley Diary.

76. "Seventh," *Western Reserve Chronicle*; Staats, *Seventh Ohio*, 88; September 16, 1862 entry, Smalley Diary; Knutson, *Took a Notion*, 3.

77. "Seventh," *Western Reserve Chronicle*; September 16, 1862 entry, Smalley Diary.

78. Ray, "Journal," 65; Staats, *Seventh Ohio*, 88–89; September 17, 1862 entry, Smalley Diary.

79. "Eugene Powell to T.W. Powell, September 18, 1862," in "The Sixty-Sixth in Another Battle," *Urbana Union* (Urbana, Ohio), October 1, 1862; United States War Department, *War of the Rebellion*, 19:938.

80. "Seventh," *Western Reserve Chronicle*; Staats, *Seventh Ohio*, 88–89.

81. Staats, *Seventh Ohio*, 88–89; "Seventh," *Western Reserve Chronicle*; September 17, 1862 entry, Smalley Diary; "Powell to Powell," *Urbana Union*.

82. Staats, *Seventh Ohio*, 88–89; "Seventh," *Western Reserve Chronicle*.

83. Ray, "Journal," 65; Staats, *Seventh Ohio*, 90; "Seventh," *Western Reserve Chronicle*; United States War Department, *War of the Rebellion*, 19:506–7.

84. "Robert S. Bower to the *Jeffersonian Democrat*, September 18, 1862," in "Our Military Correspondence," *Jeffersonian Democrat* (Chardon, OH), October 3, 1862; September 17, 1862 entry, Smalley Diary; United States War Department, *War of the Rebellion*, 19:506–7.

85. Ray, "Journal," 65; "Seventh," *Western Reserve Chronicle*; "Herbert Smalley to Gray, September 18, 1862," in "Army Correspondence: From the Seventh Ohio Regiment," *Painesville* (OH) *Telegraph*, October 2, 1862.

86. Staats, *Seventh Ohio*, 90; "From the Seventh Ohio," *Cleveland Daily Leader*, October 2, 1862.

87. Congressional Medal of Honor Society, "Murphy."

88. Staats, *Seventh Ohio*, 91; "Bower to *Jeffersonian Democrat*," *Jeffersonian Democrat*; "Smalley to Gray," *Painesville* (OH) *Telegraph*; "Seventh Ohio," *Cleveland Daily Leader*.

89. "Smalley to Gray," *Painesville* (OH) *Telegraph*; United States War Department, *War of the Rebellion*, 19:506–7.

Chapter 3

90. Galwey, *Valiant Hours*, 36; Sawyer, *Military History*, 73–74.

91. Galwey, *Valiant Hours*, 36.

92. Eicher and Eicher, *High Commands*, 470.

93. Galwey, *Valiant Hours*, 37; Sawyer, *Military History*, 74.

94. Thomas M. Ebright, "Letter from Dr. Ebright," *Holmes County Farmer* (Millersburg, OH), October 9, 1862; Galwey, *Valiant Hours*, 37–38.

95. Nickerson, "Antietam," 343; Sawyer, *Military History*, 75.

96. Nickerson, "Antietam," 343–44.

97. Ibid., 344; Galwey, *Valiant Hours*, 38.

98. Galwey, *Valiant Hours*, 37–38.

99. Ibid., 38; Sawyer, *Military History*, 76.

100. Sawyer, *Military History*, 76.

101. Galwey, *Valiant Hours*, 39; United States War Department, *War of the Rebellion*, 19:329–30.

102. United States War Department, *War of the Rebellion*, 19:329–30.

103. Masters, "Sunken Road."

104. Carman, *Antietam*, 252; Benjamin F. Ogle, "Camp on the Battlefield Near the Potomac, Maryland, September 18, 1862," *Tiffin Weekly Tribune*, October 10, 1862, 1.

105. Masters, "Sunken Road"; Daniel Lewis, "Bolivar Heights, Harper's Ferry, Virginia, September 24, 1862," *Bucyrus Journal*, October 10, 1862, 1; Carman, *Antietam*, 253.

106. "Eighth Ohio at the Battle of Antietam," *Fremont Journal*, September 26, 1862.

107. *Sandusky History*, "Letters."

108. Galwey, *Valiant Hours*, 41–43; William Kinney, "Letter from Captain Kinney—The Loss in the Eighth Ohio," *Cleveland Plain Dealer*, September 22, 1862.

109. Sawyer, *Military History*, 79.

110. Nickerson, "Antietam," 345.

111. Sawyer, *Military History*, 79.

112. Ibid., 79–80.

113. Elijah Hayden, "Death of Sergeant A.D. West," *Elyria Independent Democrat*, October 1, 1862.

114. Matthew Manly, "Second Regiment," in Clark, *North Carolina in the Great War*, 167–68; Peter Robb, "Ottawa Regiment Sends 'Priceless' Civil War Sword Home," *Ottawa Citizen*, June 2, 2020, www.ottawacitizen.com.

115. Sawyer, *Military History*, 81; "The Hibernian Guards," *Daily Cleveland Herald*, September 27, 1862; Galwey, *Valiant Hours*, 81.

116. United States War Department, *War of the Rebellion*, 19:330.

Chapter 4

117. *Mahoning Register*, September 25, 1862; "Kenney to 'Friend Joe,'" *Daily Empire*; Lyle, *Lights and Shadows*, 138.

118. Carman, *South Mountain*, 406; "Kenney to 'Friend Joe,'" *Daily Empire*; Lyle, *Lights and Shadows*, 148.

119. Cox, *April 1861–November 1863*, 305; Horton and Teverbaugh, *Eleventh Regiment*, 75.

120. Horton and Teverbaugh, *Eleventh Regiment*, 74; Lyle, *Lights and Shadows*, 149–50.

121. United States War Department, *War of the Rebellion*, 19:419, 424.

122. Ibid., 19:424, 471–72; "The Cases of Lieut. John Simpson and S. L. Christie, Aid-de-Camp," *New York Tribune*, September 16, 1862; Cunningham and Miller, *Report*, 92–93; M. Schmitt, *General George Crook*, 97.

123. Cunningham and Miller, *Report*, 92; United States War Department, *War of the Rebellion*, 19:471–73; Carman, *Antietam*, 412.

124. Carman, *Antietam*, 412; United States War Department, *War of the Rebellion*, 19:473.

125. M. Schmitt, *General George Crook*, 98; Cox, *April 1861–November 1863*, 342; Carman, *Antietam*, 412.

126. Carman, *Antietam*, 417, 421; M. Schmitt, *General George Crook*, 98; United States War Department, *War of the Rebellion*, 19:472; "The howitzer was one we had captured in West Virginia," said Cox, "and had been added to the battery, "which was partly made up of heavy rifled Parrott guns." (Jacob D. Cox, "The Battle of Antietam," in *Battles and Leaders*, 652.) Despite the early failure of Crook's brigade to seize the bridge, Colonel Henry Benning, who led the Confederate bridge defenders, credited the direct attack on the bridge, a lack of ammunition and federal troops fording the creek "above and below" the bridge. This indicates that Crook's five companies, along with the other factors, eventually played a role in carrying the bridge (United States War Department, *War of the Rebellion*, 51:163).

127. Carman, *Antietam*, 421.

128. Ibid., 447.

129. Cunningham and Miller, *Report*, 91; Mollohan, *Lincoln's Army*, 319–20.

130. Carman, *Antietam*, 486–87.

131. Ibid., 582; United States War Department, *War of the Rebellion*, 19:198.

132. Mollohan, *Lincoln's Army*, 313.

Chapter 5

133. "'Watts,'" *Cleveland Plain Dealer*; Compton, "Autobiography," 97.

134. United States War Department, *War of the Rebellion*, 19:187.

135. Warner, *Generals in Blue*, 146–47; Heineman, *Civil War Dynasty*, 74, 155.

136. Schweitzer Diary, 15; Carman, *South Mountain*, 406; Brinkerhoff, *Thirtieth Regiment*, 44; United States War Department, *War of the Rebellion*, 19:465. William Bowers was later discharged from the army because of his wounds. David Taylor rests today in Grave No. 1361 in Antietam National Cemetery. See *Official Roster of the Soldiers of the State of Ohio*, 3:420; Stotelmyer, *Bivouacs*, 139.

137. United States War Department, *War of the Rebellion*, 19:470; Carman, *Antietam*, 414, 425–28; Brinkerhoff, *Thirtieth Regiment*, 45; Compton, "Autobiography," 103; United States War Department, *War of the Rebellion*, 19:466; Tom Clemens, email message to author, May 14, 2019, confirms that Ewing's Brigade did not cross at Snavely's Ford but, instead, upstream of the ford.

138. Hugh Ewing's Report to the Adjutant General's Office, October 31, 1864, M1098, RG 94, National Archives, 12.

139. "'Watts,'" *Cleveland Plain Dealer*; Edward Everett Henry letter, undated, Twenty-Third Ohio Infantry File, Antietam National Battlefield Library.

140. Carman, *Antietam*, 482; United States War Department, *War of the Rebellion*, 19:466.

141. United States War Department, *War of the Rebellion*, 19:467–68, 470.

142. Alexander Wight to Brother, September 26, 1862, Twenty-Third Ohio Infantry File, Antietam National Battlefield Library; Carman, *Antietam*, 470, 473.

143. United States War Department, *War of the Rebellion*, 19:468, 470; Carman, *Antietam*, 473–75; "'Watts,'" *Cleveland Plain Dealer*; "'Philo' to 'Ed. Register,'" *Mahoning Register*.

144. Carman, *Antietam*, 475–76.

145. Ibid., 581; United States War Department, *War of the Rebellion*, 19:198.

146. "The Twenty-Third Regiment," *Mahoning Register*, October 2, 1862, copy in Twenty-Third Ohio Infantry File, Antietam National Battlefield Library; "E.C. to the editors' leader," *Cleveland Daily Leader*; Cunningham and Miller, *Report*, 122; Stotelmyer, *Bivouacs*, 96.

147. Quoted in Heineman, *Civil War Dynasty*, 165.

Chapter 6

148. Staats, *Seventh Ohio*, 90; "Bower to *Jeffersonian Democrat*," *Jeffersonian Democrat*.

149. "Ebright," *Holmes County Farmer*.

150. "Alexander Wight to Brother, September 26, 1862," Twenty-Third Ohio Infantry File, Antietam National Battlefield Library.

151. Compton, "Autobiography," 105–6.

152. Nickerson, "Antietam," 345.

153. "Ebright," *Holmes County Farmer*.

154. Nickerson, "Antietam," 346.

155. "H.N. Spencer to 'Friend Converse,' September 29, 1862," in "Our Military Correspondence," *Jeffersonian Democrat* (Chardon, OH), October 10, 1862; Staats, *Seventh Ohio*, 90; "Ebright," *Holmes County Farmer*; "'Watts,'" *Cleveland Plain Dealer*.

156. Staats, *Seventh Ohio*, 91.

157. "Seventh," *Western Reserve Chronicle*; "John Hume to 'Friend Day,' September 21, 1862," in Seventh Ohio Infantry File, Antietam National Battlefield Library.

158. Galwey, *Valiant Hours*, 47.

Chapter 7

159. Journal 13, July 21, 1862–September 24, 1862, box 2A, folder 4, David Hunter Strother, Artist, Artwork and Papers, A&M.2894, West Virginia and Regional History Center, www.archives.lib.wvu.edu; Schmidt, "Battlefield Burials."

160. Stotelmyer, *Bivouacs*, 20.

161. Ibid., 21.

162. Downey, Antietam.

163. Ibid.

164. Ibid.

165. Ibid.

166. Brinkerhoff, *Thirtieth Regiment*, 44.

167. Yankee Ancestry, "Dead."

168. There may very well be remains at this grave site as well. Further investigative studies will need to be done, particularly an examination of records of the removal of the dead and early cemetery superintendent reports ("Lieutenant Lantry's Remains," *Cleveland Daily Leader*, September 30, 1862).

169. Downey, Antietam.

170. Ibid.

171. Field Records of Hospitals, record group 94, entry 544, National Archives, Washington, D.C.; Lem Gentry, "The Antietam Hospital, Correspondence of the Daily State Sentinel," *Indiana Weekly Sentinel*, January 26, 1863; W.R. Mosely to J.J. Milhau, November 14, 1862, record group 94, E.623, file D, box 1, National Archives, Washington, D.C.

172. Downey, Antietam.

173. Barnes, *Medical and Surgical History*, 77.

174. Ibid.

Chapter 8

175. Thomas F. Galwey, "At the Battle of Antietam with the Eighth Ohio Infantry," in Blakeman, *Personal Recollections*, 70.

176. Cunningham and Miller, *Report*, 18–19.

177. Ibid., 22.

178. Ibid., 103.

179. Ibid., 105, 111–12.

180. Ibid., 115–17.

181. Ibid., 121–22, 125, 137.

182. Ibid., 139, 145.

183. Ibid., 149.

Conclusion

184. Burke, "Sergeant Nimrod Burke."

185. Basler, *Abraham Lincoln*, 28–30; Burke, "Sergeant Nimrod Burke."

186. Williams, *1861–1865*, 361.

187. Collins, *Army of the Potomac*, 84.

188. "Kenney to 'Friend Joe,'" *Daily Empire*; "Hay to 'Friend Estill,'" *Holmes County Farmer*; "Ebright," *Holmes County Farmer*.

Appendix

189. "William McKinley," *Ohio Archaeological and Historical Quarterly*, 233.

190. Butler, *Youngstown*, 549; "William McKinley," *Ohio Archaeological and Historical Quarterly*, 233.

191. Olcott, *William McKinley*, 22.

192. John A. Harvey to C.B. Lower, January 18, 1897, quoted in Armstrong, *Major McKinley*, 39.

193. James M. Comly to Rutherford B. Hayes, October 5, 1862, quoted in Armstrong, *Major McKinley*, 40–41.

BIBLIOGRAPHY

MANUSCRIPTS

Antietam National Battlefield Library

Seventh Ohio Infantry File
Eleventh Ohio Infantry File
Twenty-Third Ohio Infantry File

Gilder Lehrman Collection

Diary of Herbert L. Smalley, GLC00653.14

National Archives, Washington, D.C.

Field Records of Hospitals, entry 544, record group 94
U.S. Army Generals' Reports of Civil War Service, M1098, record group 94

BIBLIOGRAPHY

New York Public Library

Ezra Carman Papers, Manuscripts and Archives Division, MSS-473

Ohio Historical Society

Governor's Official Papers, Letters Received

Rubenstein Library, Duke University

Samuel Wilson Compton Papers

United States Army Heritage and Education Center

Civil War Times Illustrated Collection of Civil War Papers
Edward E. Schweitzer Diary (Thirtieth Ohio Infantry)

West Virginia and Regional History Center

David Hunter Strother, Artist, Artwork and Papers

NEWSPAPERS

Bucyrus Journal
Cleveland Daily Leader
Cleveland Plain Dealer
Daily Cleveland Herald
Daily Empire
Elyria Independent Democrat
Fremont Journal
Herald and Torch Light
Holmes County Farmer
Indiana Weekly Sentinel
Jeffersonian Democrat
Mahoning Register
New York Herald
New York Tribune
Ottawa Citizen
Painesville Telegraph
Tiffin Weekly Tribune
Urbana Union
Western Reserve Chronicle

PUBLISHED WORKS

Armstrong, William H. *Major McKinley: William McKinley & the Civil War.* Kent, OH: Kent State University Press, 2000.

Barnes, Joseph K. *The Medical and Surgical History of the War of the Rebellion.* Washington, D.C.: U.S. Government Printing Office, 1870.

Basler, Roy. P, ed. *The Collected Works of Abraham Lincoln.* Vol. 6. New Brunswick, NJ: Rutgers University Press, 1953.

Battles and Leaders of the Civil War. Vol. 2. New York: Century Co., 1887.

Beyer, Walter F., and Oscar F. Keydel. *Deeds of Valor: How America's Heroes Won the Medal of Honor.* Vol. 1. Detroit, MI: Perrien-Keydel Company, 1901.

Blakeman, Alexander Noel, ed. *Personal Recollections of the War of the Rebellion: Addresses Delivered Before the Commandery of the State of New York, Military Order of the Loyal Legion of the United States.* New York: G.P. Putnam's Sons, 1907.

Brinkerhoff, Henry R. *History of the Thirtieth Regiment Ohio Volunteer Infantry, from Its Organization, to the Fall of Vicksburg, Miss.* Columbus, OH: James W. Osgood, 1863.

Burke, Henry Robert. "Sergeant Nimrod Burke." Lest We Forget. www.lestweforget.hamptonu.edu.

Butler, Joseph Green, Jr. *History of Youngstown and the Mahoning Valley Ohio.* Chicago: American Historical Society, 1921.

Card, Nan. "Lucy Hayes' Visit to Wounded Ohioans after the Battle of South Mountain Md." *Ohio Civil War Genealogy Journal* 16, no. 3 (September 2012): 144–45.

Carman, Ezra A. *Antietam.* Edited by Thomas G. Clemens. Vol. 2 of *The Maryland Campaign of September 1862.* New York: Savas Beatie, 2012.

———. *South Mountain.* Edited by Thomas G. Clemens. Vol. 1 of *The Maryland Campaign of September 1862.* New York: Savas Beatie, 2010.

Clark, Walter, ed. *Histories of the Several Regiments and Battalions from North Carolina in the Great War 1861–65, Written by Members of the Respective Commands.* Vol. 1. Raleigh, NC: N.p., 1901.

Coles, Harry L. *Ohio Forms an Army.* Columbus: Ohio State University Press, 1962.

Collins, Darrell L. *The Army of the Potomac: Order of Battle, 1861–1865, with Commanders, Strengths, Losses and More.* Jefferson, NC: McFarland & Company, 2013.

Congressional Medal of Honor Society. "John P. Murphy." www.cmohs.org.

Cox, Jacob Dolson. *April 1861–November 1863.* Vol. 1 of *Reminiscences of the Civil War.* New York: Charles Scribner's Sons, 1900.

Cunningham, D., and W.W. Miller. *Report of the Ohio Antietam Battlefield Commission*. Springfield, OH: Springfield Publishing Company, 1904.

Downey, Brian. Antietam on the Web. www.antietam.aotw.org.

Dyer, Frederick H. *A Compendium of the War of the Rebellion*. 2 vols. Dayton, OH: Morningside Press, 1994.

Eicher, David J., and John H. Eicher. *Civil War High Commands*. Stanford, CA: Stanford University Press, 2001.

Fritsch, James T. *The Untried Life: The Twenty-Ninth Ohio Volunteer Infantry in the Civil War*. Athens: Swallow Press/Ohio University Press, 2012.

Galwey, Thomas Francis. *The Valiant Hours*. Edited by W.S. Nye. Harrisburg, PA: Stackpole Company, 1961.

Harper, Robert S. *Ohio Handbook of the Civil War*. Columbus: Ohio Historical Society, 1961.

Hartwig, D. Scott. *To Antietam Creek: The Maryland Campaign of September 1862*. Baltimore, MD: Johns Hopkins University Press, 2012.

Heineman, Kenneth J. *Civil War Dynasty: The Ewing Family of Ohio*. New York: New York University Press, 2013.

Hoptak, John David. *The Battle of South Mountain*. Charleston, SC: The History Press, 2011.

Horton, Joshua H., and Solomon Teverbaugh. *A History of the Eleventh Regiment, Ohio Volunteer Infantry*. Dayton, OH: W.J. Shuey, 1866.

In Memoriam: George Sears Greene, Brevet Major-General, United States Volunteers, 1801–1899. Albany, NY: J.B. Lyon Company, 1909.

Johnson, Curt, and Richard C. Anderson Jr. *Artillery Hell: The Employment of Artillery at Antietam*. College Station: Texas A&M University Press, 1995.

Kepler, William. *History of the Three Months' and Three Years' Service of the Fourth Regiment Ohio Volunteer Infantry in the War for the Union*. Cleveland, OH: Leader Printing Company, 1886.

Knutson, Anne Baxter, ed. *Took a Notion: The Civil War Diaries of William Henry Baxter of Mechanicsburg, Ohio*. Afton, MN: Anne Baxter Knutson, 1995.

Lyle, W.W. *Lights and Shadows of Army Life*. Cincinnati, OH: R.W. Carroll & Co., 1865.

Masters, Dan. "Taking the Sunken Road: The Eighth Ohio at Antietam." *Dan Masters' Civil War Chronicles*. June 20, 2020. www.dan-masters-civil-war.blogspot.com.

Mollohan, Marie. *Another Day in Lincoln's Army: The Civil War Journals of Sgt. John T. Booth*. Lincoln, NE: iUniverse Inc., 2007.

Nickerson, A.H. "Antietam — A Reminiscence." *Blue and Gray* 2 (1893): 343–47.

Official Roster of the Soldiers of the State of Ohio in the War of the Rebellion, 1861–1866. 12 vols. Cincinnati, OH: Ohio Valley Pub. & Mfg. Co., 1886.

Olcott, Charles S. *The Life of William McKinley.* Vol. 1. Boston: Houghton Mifflin Company, 1916.

"President William McKinley: Main Events in His Life." *Ohio Archaeological and Historical Quarterly* 10, no. 2 (1902): 232–35.

Ray, George B. "Journal of George B. Ray." *Historical and Philosophical Society of Ohio*, 1926, 57–73.

Sandusky History. "Letters from the Front." October 10, 2007. www.sanduskyhistory.blogspot.com.

Sawyer, Franklin. *A Military History of the 8th Regiment Ohio Vol. Inf'y: Its Battles, Marches and Army Movements.* Cleveland, OH: Fairbanks & Co. Printers, 1881.

Schmidt, Allan. "Battlefield Burials After Antietam." *Antietam Journal.* October 22, 2013. www.antietamjournal.blogspot.com.

Schmitt, Martin F., ed. *General George Crook: His Autobiography.* Norman: University of Oklahoma Press, 1960.

Staats, Richard J. *The Bully Seventh Ohio Volunteer Infantry.* Vol. 2 of *A Grassroots History of the American Civil War.* Bowie, MD: Heritage Books Inc., 2003.

Stotelmyer, Steven R. *The Bivouacs of the Dead: The Story of Those Who Died at Antietam and South Mountain.* Baltimore, MD: Toomey Press, 1992.

———. *Too Useful to Sacrifice: Reconsidering George B. McClellan's Generalship in the Maryland Campaign from South Mountain to Antietam.* El Dorado Hills, CA: Savas Beatie, 2019.

Thorp, Gene M., and Alexander B. Rossino. *The Tale Untwisted: George McClellan and the Discovery of Lee's Lost Orders, September 13, 1862.* El Dorado Hills, CA: Savas Beatie, 2019.

United States War Department. *The War of the Rebellion: A Compilation of the Official Records of the Union and Confederate Armies.* 128 vols. Washington, D.C.: GPO, 1880–1901.

Ward, J.E.D. *Twelfth Ohio Volunteer Inf.* Ripley, OH: N.p., 1864.

Warner, Ezra J. *Generals in Blue: Lives of the Union Commanders.* Baton Rouge: Louisiana State University Press, 1964.

Williams, Charles Richard, ed. *1861–1865.* Vol. 2 of *Diary and Letters of Rutherford Birchard Hayes.* Columbus: Ohio State Archaeological and Historical Society, 1922.

Yankee Ancestry. "Concord's Civil War Dead." January 15, 2007. www.yankeeancestry.tripod.com.

Index

ABOUT THE AUTHORS

Dan Welch is an educator with a public school district in Northeast Ohio. Dan continues to serve as a seasonal park ranger at Gettysburg National Military Park. He received a bachelor's degree in instrumental music education from Youngstown State University and a master's degree in military history with a Civil War–era concentration from American Military University. He has been a contributing member at *Emerging Civil War* for over six years and is the coauthor of *The Last Road North: A Guide to the Gettysburg Campaign, 1863*. He resides with his wife, Sarah, in Boardman, Ohio.

Kevin Pawlak is a historic site manager for Prince William County's Office of Historic Preservation and serves as a certified battlefield guide at Antietam National Battlefield and Harpers Ferry National Historical Park. He graduated from Shepherd University in 2014 with a degree in history with a concentration in Civil War and nineteenth-century America and a minor in historic preservation. Kevin is a regular contributor to *Emerging Civil War*. He is also the author of three books on the Maryland Campaign, including two with Arcadia Publishing and The History Press.

Visit us at
www.historypress.com